One Monday in November
... and beyond

Gates at the rear of Headley Grange

One Monday in November

... *and beyond*

෨෨෨

The Story of the Selborne & Headley Workhouse Riots of 1830

... *and their aftermath*

෨෨෨

John Owen Smith

One Monday in November ... and Beyond

First published September 2002

Includes material previously published in *One Monday in November*,
May 1993

Typeset and published by John Owen Smith
19 Kay Crescent, Headley Down, Hampshire GU35 8AH

Tel/Fax: 01428 712892
wordsmith@headley-village.com
www.headley-village.com/wordsmith

ISBN 1-873855-33-8

[Replacing ISBN 1-873855-09-5]

Printed and bound by Antony Rowe Ltd, Eastbourne

Publisher's Note

In this new edition, we have retained the text of the original publication (which had no need for updating), and added information gathered subsequently about the circumstances of the rioters and their families after the trials—information obtained largely from their direct descendants.

There is also additional material relating to events and commemorations which have happened since the original publication, and details of a 'Rioters Walk' from Selborne to Headley and back again, for you to follow on foot if you wish.

To my parents, Doreen and Les,
whose fascination for history
I seem to have inherited

Contents

Illustrations & Maps

Foreword

Jo Smith's book is a real contribution to our history. It tells the story of a few tragic days in East Hampshire in 1830, when hungry men, bewildered by falling wages and rising prices, blundered into mob action. They wrecked two buildings, in a period when property was sacred – and retribution was savage – but strangely selective.

1830 – fifteen years since Waterloo and the defeat of revolutionary France, but years of depression and city riots! Now it was the turn of the countryside, where the hardships of the poor had been increased by low wages, enclosures and new machinery. In August the farm-workers of Kent suddenly broke out in riot and destruction. Mobs roamed the countryside carrying banners inscribed 'Bread or Blood,' demanding money, firing ricks and destroying machines. Could England too be drifting towards revolution? The flame spread rapidly westwards. Our turn came in late November. The disturbances in Selborne and Headley were closely connected – in time, targets and cast of characters. In Liphook itself the mob was dispersed by firm action – but Liphook men almost certainly joined in the violence at Headley. In Jo Smith's book the events in the three villages are at last told as one coherent story.

I am particularly happy to have the chance to introduce the book to the public. A few years ago I researched and wrote a brief account of the riots, so I am probably one of the few people who can appreciate fully how hard Mr Smith must have worked, how thorough and widespread his investigations have been, unearthing ten times more information than I found. He gives us the economic and social background and then recounts the facts, with clarity, humour and impartiality. His sympathies are clear, but he has not made all his rich men villains or all his poor men saints; he has told it "as it happened." Selborne, Headley and Liphook are much in his debt.

Laurence C Giles
Vice-Chairman, Bramshott and Liphook Preservation Society, 1993

View east across The Plestor, Selborne, late C18
(Vicarage out of picture behind wall on the left)

Author's Note

In 1992 I was asked by East Hampshire District Council to write a playscript on the subject of the Selborne workhouse riot of 1830. Since I live in the neighbouring village of Headley, I was well aware that we'd also had a workhouse riot in the same year, and rumour said the people who did it came from Selborne. "Typical!" I thought. I knew very little more than that, but it seemed to me that it would be interesting, and still within the terms of East Hampshire's brief, to trace the connection between the two events in the play.

So began what seemed like a never-ending trail of fact-finding, matching and interpreting, as more and more interviews, visits, reading and re-reading produced ever more conflicting evidence and ambiguity. Eventually a story emerged which differed in some important and interesting aspects from that which local legends had previously suggested.

Then I had to shoe-horn the facts into a script, remembering that plays must also entertain as well as educate. Inevitably many compromises had to be made: invented dialogue was written to make the characters come alive on the stage, and many hard-gained pieces of information which would have lengthened the play without adding to its dramatic effect were excluded. The play was therefore not a strictly accurate record of the facts.

So in order to redress the balance, I decided to publish a more complete account of the collected information in book form, and *One Monday in November* was the result.

What I believed I had done for the first time was to pull together the known information on two truly dramatic November days and their aftermath in a particular way. However, I was quite unprepared for an aftermath of a different kind.

I was writing about events which had occurred over 160 years previously, and I thought I was therefore fairly safe from any come-back by those involved. But I had not bargained for the growing world-wide interest in genealogy.

Since publishing that first book, I have been contacted by the families of no fewer than a dozen of the named rioters—and it is an eerie sensation to answer the telephone in the middle of an afternoon and be told that you are speaking to the great-great-granddaughter of the man transported for leading the riots.

She, and several of the others, had not previously been aware of a connection with these events—and in some cases there were relations on the other side of the world who those contacting me knew nothing about. In fact, over the past seven years I have sometimes felt like the organiser of a 'lonely hearts club', putting one side of a family in touch with the other. This was an unexpected outcome from what, to me, had initially been just a local community project—but, it has to be said, a most rewarding one.

So now, not only can you follow our band of local men as they marched along the lanes and tracks through this part of East Hampshire in 1830 to do what they could to relieve their poverty, but also read on and see what became of them and their descendants afterwards—information not available in the first publication.

I hope you find it as fascinating to read as I did to write.

John Owen Smith
Headley, AD 2002

One Monday in November ...

... in the year 1830, a mob several hundred strong attacked the workhouse in Selborne, Hampshire, turned out the occupants, burned or broke the fittings and furniture, and pulled down the roof. The next day an even larger mob, containing some of the Selborne rioters, did the same to the workhouse at Headley, some seven miles away. The parsons in both villages were also coerced into promising to reduce by half the income they took from tithes.

Less than a month later, at a special court hearing in Winchester attended by no less a person than the Duke of Wellington, nine local men were sentenced to transportation (commuted from a death sentence in the case of eight of them), and all but one sailed for the antipodes in the Spring of 1831 never to return.

These are the bare bones of the story. But why did the riot start? Why were the two workhouses attacked? And why were some of the supporters and leaders of the mobs seen to be not oppressed labourers, but relatively well-to-do artisans and farmers?

In this book we cover the dramatic events of the two days and their aftermath, piecing together the sometimes contradictory reports and legends which have grown up during intervening years around the names and deeds of those involved in the action.

ᘓᘓᘓ

Parish of Headley.

To Mr. THOMAS MARNER WALKER, and FRANCIS BRYANT, Guardians of the Poor of the Parish of Headley, in the County of Southampton, and to each of them.

WE, the undersigned, Daniel Knight, (Collecting Overseer,) Robert Parker, John Clear, William Swann, Edward Keen, George Baker, John Fisher, and Richard Knight, Junr. Occupiers of Messuages, Lands, Tenements, and Hereditaments, rated and rateable to the Poor, in the said Parish of Headley, Do hereby give you and each of you Notice, that We are willing and desirous of employing Paupers in the Parish, at the Wages of Six Shillings per Week each, being fair and reasonable Wages at this Time, when the Price of Corn is very low, and the Bread is consequently cheap; and that the receipt of Money for Agricultural Produce by Farmers is so much reduced, that no one can pay more for common Labour than at the rate of Six Shillings per Week; and for as much as you, or one of you, as Guardians of the Poor of Headley, have lately been in the habit of employing many of the Labourers on the Highways, and otherwise, at Wages of Eight Shillings a Week, from the Money collected on the Poor Rates, We consider ourselves aggrieved, because the Poor Rates are thereby greatly increased, to the grievous Injury of ourselves and all those who pay Poor Rates in the Parish!

We conceive that you have no just or lawful Right thus to burden those who pay the Poor Rates, by employing the Paupers at high Wages, whilst there is Employ for them at less Wages in the Agricultural Matters in the Parish, and We declare that it will be utterly impossible for us to pay the Poor Rates, thus raised by you, with our diminished means of paying them, and that the System you have adopted of employing Labourers heretofore employed in Husbandry, and other Matters, at higher Wages than a Farmer can afford to pay, is in every way ruinous in the extreme to the greatest part, if not the whole of the Occupiers of Land in the Parish.

This is therefore to give you Notice, and to caution you, that We shall jointly and severally resist, and We do hereby protest against your pursuing the said System in future; and that We will hereafter jointly or severally appeal against your Accounts, as Guardians and Overseers of the Poor, if the high Wages before-mentioned be given and charged in your Accounts, whilst We are ready and willing to employ the Poor at reasonable and fair Wages as aforesaid; and We give you further Notice, that you have no Right to employ the Paupers at the Expence of the Poor Rates, whilst they can get Employ elsewhere in the Parish.---And We give you Notice also to get your Accounts verified before a Magistrate once a Month;† and passed by the Visitor once a Quarter, as required by the Statute of 22 Geo. III. Chap. 83. And We beg to assure you, We hold no hostile Disposition or Ill-will against you or either of you; at the same Time We are driven to the Necessity of taking Measures, to prevent so great an Evil and Loss as before stated.

Dated this Twenty-eighth Day of May, 1822.

D. Knight,	John Clear,	William Swann,	Richard Knight, Jun.
Robert Parker,	John Fisher,	George Baker,	Edward Keen.

— ✳ *Collecting Overseer*

† N.B. This is a Mistake. By the Statute of 22. Geo. III. Chap. 83. the Accounts of the Guardians are to be verified, not once a Month, but once a Quarter.

J. B. RUTTER, PRINTER, FARNHAM.

Poster issued by farmers of Headley in May 1822

Background

After Waterloo

Like 1066, the year 1815 is one which is well known to most scholars, and generally assumed to be a 'good thing'—the final victory over Napoleon by the allies at Waterloo. But this victory, and the ensuing peace in Europe, was the beginning of the end as far as the English agricultural labourer was concerned.

There had already been a steady move by law-makers and large land-owners in the country away from supporting the traditional land-owning peasant, able to grow some of his own food and keep a few animals, towards using the wage-earning labourer who had no land of his own and relied entirely for subsistence on the money he earned. During the Napoleonic wars, labour was scarce and wages therefore relatively high, but after Waterloo, returning soldiers swelled the available workforce, and labour was no longer at a premium.

Problems of falling wages and rising prices inevitably led to discontent, and in some cases abject poverty among the labourers and their dependants, and so-called 'bread or blood' riots broke out in East Anglia and elsewhere. By the time the autumn of 1830 came round, some particularly bad harvests in the previous two summers and a severe winter in between had set the scene for another period of agitation. But now there were other influences which made the uprisings more significant than before.

Across the Channel, revolutions were still occurring in France, and also in Belgium which gained its independence from Holland in November of that year. In Britain, King George IV died during the summer, his brother William succeeded to the throne, and a general election changed the government from Tory to Whig for the first time in many years. So a new, untried administration was looking nervously across the water at a Europe once again in turmoil, and seeing any signs of local revolt in this country as a possible start to a larger and more serious civil conflict.

But such unrest had been predicted earlier in the year, when William Cobbett reflected that he would "better be a dog than a farmer next winter." And when the traditional 'doling' period of the year arrived, that time between the end of harvest and the start of the new year when the labourer's work is at its minimum and consequently he has more time in which to reflect on his lack of earnings, the customary gatherings and perambulations of labourers to exact money and food from the better-off villagers turned into something altogether more serious.

Starting in Kent during the early autumn these disturbances, which have become known as the 'Swing Riots,' swept across southern England and reached Hampshire in the second week of November. Nobody quite knows how the movement spread, but at the time the government convinced itself that it was the work of French spies, or travelling Methodist ministers, or a plot co-ordinated by a self-styled 'Captain Swing,' whose name was at the bottom of some of the posters and threatening letters which began to appear. They could not believe simply that the circumstances of the village labourer, and to a degree the village tradesmen and small farmers, had become so unbearable that word of a riot succeeding and forcing an increase in wages and a reduction of rates in one village would be enough to spark a 'copy cat' rising in the next.

The actions taken by rioters differed from place to place, depending on local circumstances and local grievances. In many locations threshing machines, first introduced in the 1780s but now becoming more widespread, were seen to be taking away the winter livelihood of the labourer and became a target. In other places parsons were mobbed and forced to sign agreements to take less in tithes from the land, or magistrates urged to declare a general raise in wages in their area. Selborne and Headley were almost unique in that, along with the more common actions, the mobs also ransacked the workhouses (poor houses) there.

Selborne in 1830

Selborne was not a happy place during this period. William Cobbett, when staying there overnight on one of his 'Rural Rides' in 1823, reported that he met a local man who told him that "he did not believe there was a more unhappy place in England" than Selborne. When asked why, he replied that "there's always quarrels of some sort or other going on ... on matters of rates and tithes mostly." Cobbett then remembered he had read about a shot being fired through the vicar's window, and a King's proclamation for a reward relating to the discovery of the perpetrator. Nobody came forward to claim the reward.

The vicar in question, William Rust Cobbold, was not well loved in his parish. He was regarded as arrogant by his parishioners, and on his own admission seemed to be in constant conflict with his vestry. For a parish which could still remember the gentle curacy of Gilbert White, this must have been an unhappy situation indeed. We have records of acrimonious notes passing between him and the officials of the parish, and of court actions taken by him and them. Following the events of 1830 he acquired a mastiff dog with a neck 'as thick as a lion's' for his protection; its collar can be seen to this day in the church.

The vestry would meet in the public house, where they "knew the vicar would not go," he claiming to be the "only gentleman in the village." It is therefore perhaps not surprising to find that the ex-landlord of this pub, who had been expelled from this position by Cobbold and who some sources say was a member of the Selborne vestry, played a leading role in the events which unfolded in the village and spilt over into neighbouring parishes.

Headley in 1830

By contrast the rector at Headley, described as a "jolly, big old Cumbrian farmer who suffered from ill-health and was a good deal absent from the village," seems to have been regarded in a more kindly light by his flock. He was present in the village at the time of the riot, and the difference between his attitude and that of the vicar of Selborne can be seen by the fact that he was prepared to attend a meeting in the village pub to discuss labourers wages.

Although as a bald statement of fact similar events happened in Headley as in Selborne, the parson was 'mobbed' to reduce his tithes and the workhouse was sacked, the actions here seem to have been directed less at personalities and more at the institutions they represented.

That is not to say there were no differences of opinion in Headley—what village could exist without them? There was, for example, a public poster-debate in 1822 between certain small farmers of the parish and the Guardians of the Poor as to what should be regarded as 'fair and reasonable' labourers' wages. The small farmers thought six shillings a week for a labourer over 20 years of age was adequate, while the Guardians thought eight or nine shillings more reasonable. In 1830 the cry was for twelve shillings, but we have records from 1843 showing that nine shillings continued to be the going rate in Headley.

Village Finances

Since the whole argument of the riots was over money, it is important to understand the social and financial structure of a village at that time.

At the top of the tree there was normally a large landowner, possibly a Lord of the Manor, to whom the majority of the villagers and the parson would owe allegiance. But in Selborne and Headley this was not the case; neither village had a resident Lord of the Manor nor a significant single landowner at that time. Hobsbawm and Rudé in their book *Captain Swing* tend to see the lack of such a restraining influence as being one of the factors making a village susceptible to riot.

The Tithes

The parson in a village lived on the tithes which were due to him from the parish, plus the proceeds of any other activity he might pursue or land he might possess. Tithes were originally introduced as long ago as 750 AD, being payable in kind as a tenth *(= tithe)* of the produce of the land to the 'tithe-holder'. In the case of a Rector, he was due both the 'great' or rectorial tithes (corn, beans, peas, hay and wood) and the 'small' or vicarial tithes (the remainder); a Vicar was only due the small tithes, the great tithes going to some other holder—in the case of Selborne, to Magdalen College, Oxford.

The massive tithe barns which still exist around the country were built to store the corn, hay, wood and other commodities due to the church each year. But it was always a problem for the parson or tithe-holder physically to collect such tithes, particularly if landowners were reluctant to deliver and he had to arrange himself for the produce to be brought in. Roads in those days, it must be remembered, were still dirt tracks and often ankle deep or worse in mud. So by 1830 it had become common practice for the Church to collect tithes in money, at an agreed exchange rate equivalent to the value of the produce that would otherwise be due, or for them to sell the rights to 'farm the tithes' to the highest bidder.

But this sum tended to become fixed over a period of time, and not reflect the natural fluctuations of good and lean years. Thus after two poor harvests in 1829 and 1830, farmers found they still had to hand over the same amount of money to the tithe-holder as in a good year, even though they had less produce to sell in order to pay for it.

The Poor Rate

Moreover, tithes were not the only taxes due from landowners. There were also land taxes to be paid, and in addition each parish was charged with looking after its own Poor, and the funds for this were levied by applying a local Poor Rate, which was paid according to the rateable value of property. The rate was agreed periodically by officers of the parish according to their need for funds, and the definition as to who was and was not a pauper, and therefore able to claim 'on the parish,' was a point of continual argument. Real poverty, to the extent of actual starvation, was far from unknown in the rural communities of the time, and in 1795 a group of Berkshire magistrates concerned to raise labourers' wages to a subsistence level met at the Pelican Inn, Speenhamland (now part of Newbury), and made what turned out to be a momentous decision, gradually adopted across most of England.

Instead of raising wages, or more precisely fixing them to the current price of bread as had been intended, the meeting chose to supplement existing low wages from the parish fund (the Poor Rate) up to the intended figure. This decision produced almost the opposite effect to that desired. It meant that labourers could now receive a minimum wage for doing nothing, although generally the parish found work for the able-bodied to do, such as repairing roads, or hiring them out to farmers at an agreed rate. It also meant that farmers were not encouraged to pay 'reasonable' wages, since they knew the Poor Rate would pay the shortfall. *(See the Appendix on **Labour Rates in 1830** for more details)*. Granted the farmers were also among those contributing to the Poor Rate by way of taxes, but this load was shared between all the other property-owning parishioners who then begrudged the fact that they were subsidising the farmers' labour. The farmers pointed to the high tithes as an excuse for not being able to pay more.

A Report of the Poor Law Commissioners in 1835 said, *'Many farmers dismiss workers even from profitable employment to make others assist in maintaining them. They do not want to see their neighbours have a lighter burden in helping the poor.'* And in the middle of this argument, the labourers and their families saw no escape from the poverty trap. The Settlement Acts made it difficult for them to move to find better jobs (other parishes would only allow them to stay if their 'home parish' certified that they would take them back if they could not support themselves), and if they resorted to poaching, which was the only other real means of improving their lot, the penalty was transportation or death—or a maiming for life in a man-trap, which was almost as bad.

The Poor Houses

For those who had no other home, the parish provided accommodation in Poor Houses, or workhouses as they were more commonly referred to. While these were never places of ease, the original concept of having a number of small houses in which families could be kept together was at least tolerable. However, in an attempt to encourage those who could get out and work to do so, a policy began to be adopted in which paupers were brought together to live in larger 'Union' buildings which were purposely made to be cheerless and uncomfortable. In these, families would be segregated by sex and a tough regime adopted. Residents could not go out or see visitors without the permission of the Master, who was often running the workhouse on a franchise basis to make a living for himself and his family.

While a more general move to create 'Union' Houses occurred later as a result of the 1834 Poor Law, the idea had started as early as the 1770s, and Selborne and Headley (along with Alton) appear to have been forward in their thinking. The Selborne building was purchased in 1794 for £250 from James Knight, and the Headley 'House of Industry' was built in 1795 at an estimated cost of some £1,500 for the parishes of Headley, Bramshott and Kingsley, to shelter their infirm, aged paupers, and orphan or illegitimate children. To add to their degradation, all who received parish relief in Headley wore a badge on their clothing to proclaim the fact, with the metal letters 'HP' for Headley Poor.

Why the Riot?

If the tithes could be reduced, then the farmers could, in theory at least, pay the difference in higher wages to their labourers, and perhaps even take on more labour than before. This would stop the need for payment of 'parish relief' to these labourers and their families, which would then reduce the Poor Rate payments of all tax payers in the parish. In short, everyone would seem to gain from it except the clergy, and possibly the master of the Poor House who would be given less money to dispense. The main target of the villagers was therefore the Church tithes, which were seen as an unnecessary drain on parish resources, and in Selborne, at least, as going into the pocket of an unpopular man.

But the church would not give up its traditional income willingly. The only way that hard-pressed parishioners could see of achieving their aim was by using force of numbers, and as a result many vicars and rectors in the south of England were 'mobbed' during the 1830 disturbances, usually with labourers to the fore and farmers and other tax-paying tradesman urging them on from behind. In this way the labourers took the brunt of the retribution handed out in subsequent trials, even though their masters and social betters were likely to gain as much if not more than they from any reductions obtained. Of the 22 men known to have been arrested following the Selborne and Headley riots, all but three or four were agricultural labourers; Holdaway, Heath, Triggs and possibly James were the exceptions, and not one farmer was arrested.

So we can see a logical argument as to why the parishioners of a village should want to 'mob' their parson—but it is more difficult to understand why they attacked the Poor Houses. In this, Selborne and Headley were, as previously noted, almost unique. Hobsbawm & Rudé in *Captain Swing* record other instances of Overseers being attacked, but not of other Poor Houses being sacked. Certainly there would seem to have been no real benefit for the farmers, the tradesmen, or the rioters to have the Poor Houses destroyed. The short answer is, we don't know why; but it may be that other 'rioting' villages did not have such obvious, invidious and undefended targets to attack. It seems that while the crowd's blood was up in Selborne and Headley, they felt they might as well use it as an excuse to 'have a go' at the hated Union *Werk'uses*. But while this may go some way to explaining the Selborne incident, the Headley sacking appears to have been far more premeditated, and therefore less explicable in this way.

Premeditated or not, it certainly seems as though the activities of the mob got out of hand on the day. It is not clear what control either the farmers or Robert Holdaway and the other tradesmen expected to exercise over events, but as the judge said when summing up Holdaway's case, "I hope that the events of this day will mark an awful lesson to any who may hereafter think of engaging in such deeds of outrage; I hope that they will teach such persons it may be impossible to check or control the disorderly spirits whom they may have called into action to effect their own wicked and illegal purposes." We may dispute whether they were wicked, or even whether everything they were accused of was strictly illegal, but there is no doubt that where a mob of people is involved, the heart often rules the head and little account is taken by those involved at the time of what may seem sensible in retrospect.

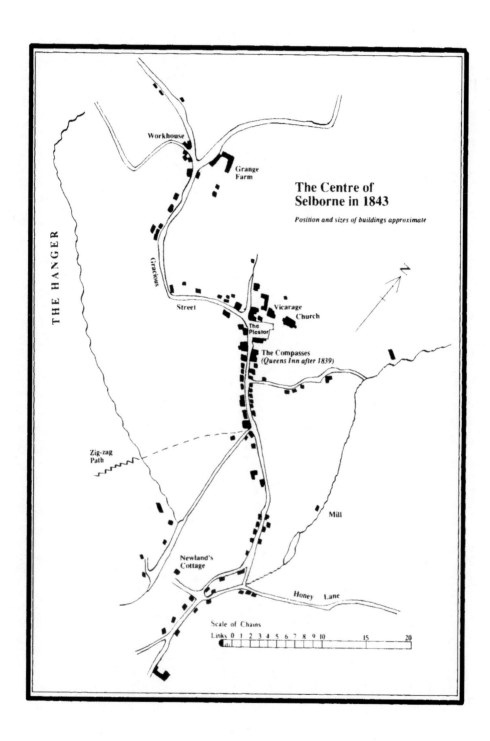

The Centre of
Selborne in 1843

Position and sizes of buildings approximate

THE HANGER

Workhouse

Grange
Farm

Gracious

Street

Vicarage
Church

The
Plestor

The Compasses
(Queens Inn after 1839)

N

Zig-zag
Path

Mill

Newland's
Cottage

Honey   Lane

Scale of Chains
Links 0 1 2 3 4 5 6 7 8 9 10   15   20

Selborne
Saturday 20th–Monday 22nd November, 1830

The Saturday Dole

On the Saturday before the disturbances, the labourers and paupers of Selborne were doled out their weekly allowance from the parish as normal. It seems that they received this from Mr John Harrison, referred to in contemporary *Times* reports as the 'guardian,' who was the Master of the Poor House there.

We are not sure whether the recipients went down to the Poor House to receive their dole, or whether it was given out to them at some other location in the village, but on this particular occasion Mr Harrison recollected that some of them "expressed their intention of going round to the farmers to make them raise their wages." He said he "advised them not to do so, or they would repent hereafter." It could have been normal banter, but later events showed that on this day the complaints held a greater significance.

However, it was not the farmers who they went round to next, but Mr Harrison himself. He was obviously not a popular man. He was referred to by Holdaway's counsel as being "particularly obnoxious to the poor of the neighbourhood," and another correspondent recalled an incident "which exited a universal feeling of disgust" when it was discovered that some of the inmates were chained to the wall. The *Times* records that "about 12 o'clock in the night of the same day three guns, loaded with slugs, were discharged into the bedroom of Mr Harrison at the workhouse, and although the clothes and furniture of the bed were completely torn to pieces by the slugs, we are happy to say none of the family were wounded."

Sunday, 21st November

It is doubtful whether the next day was a Day of Rest for many in the village, and it would be interesting to know what sermon the Reverend William Cobbold chose to read out in St Mary's church that morning. We can imagine the impromptu meetings which must have gone on as the parishioners left the south door after matins and ducked under the boughs of the old yew tree: farmers consulting each other, and walking together up the main street to *The Compasses* to finish the discussion over a beer; tradesmen and artisans likewise involved; and groups of labourers perhaps organising their own meetings away from the eye of their masters.   But this is conjecture.

We are told by James Bridger, a farmer of Oakhanger, in a letter written later at the request of William Cowburn, a London solicitor whose family lived part of the year in the village, that the farmers first heard on Sunday morning that there was to be a mob at Selborne. Hori Hale (another farmer) and Henry Collyer (a churchwarden) went to Cobbold to ask his advice, but "he was very short with them and told them they might do as they thought fit; for his part he could do nothing."

Mrs Cowburn reported that men climbed into the yew tree overlooking the vicarage on Sunday evening to make sure Cobbold would not get away in the night.

Monday Morning, Outside the Vicarage

The next thing we are told is that at seven o'clock on Monday morning Cobbold, as he left the vicarage, observed two or three of his own labourers among a group of 7 or 8 talking together. He then saw Aaron Harding join the men, and when he asked them what they were going to do Harding told him they were going to "turn out old Harrison," and that they must have their wages raised to 12 shillings a week.

Aaron Harding was a 41 year old labourer, widowed the previous year and with nine children aged between two and twenty. He was later described by the vicar as being "desperate and daring." We know from the Poor Book records that three years earlier he was receiving a dole from the parish of 12 shillings a week, made up of seven shillings for his 6 youngest children, 2/6d for his wife and 2/6d for himself, but we do not know what he was receiving at the time of the riot.

The vicar told him that he saw no objection to wages of 12 shillings a week, as he paid at least that sum to his own labourers, and "to some 14 shillings besides giving them in addition a cottage and a garden." Given his general unpopularity within the village, it seems unlikely that this would endear him further to the other employers of labour who had to fund their wage bill from the land, while Cobbold received a substantial sum in tithes from which to pay his expenses.

Bridger's letter says that the farmers had called a meeting a few days before and agreed to "advance the labourers' wages to 2/- a day," in order to prevent the sort of riots in Selborne that were happening elsewhere; however Cowburn himself declares that "the farmers deliberated, but came to no decision."

We deduce that a discussion of some sort between the farmers and labourers of Selborne must have occurred however, for Harding then said to the vicar, "We must have a touch of your tithes." Cobbold first of all seemed to treat this as a joke, stating that if his income was reduced he "could not do the good he was in the habit of doing," and pointing out to Harding that he had been particularly kind to his family, which we assume referred to the time of his bereavement the previous year. Harding was in no mood for compromise however, and said the tithes must be reduced to £300 a year, adding that this was "quite enough and according to our regulation." It is not clear whose regulation he meant, but by implication it probably came from the farmers. John Trimming (25), another of the rioters whose name we know from later committal proceedings, is reported to have added that £4 a week was quite enough for Cobbold, leaving us to wonder which was wrong, his arithmetic or our information.

The vicar must have asked who was going to persuade him to do this, for Harding then told him they had "a large party" and asked him to come and look at them. A contemporary report mentions that "a mob about 300 in number, collected from the surrounding country, had entered Selborne armed with large clubs, etc." Cobbold presumably declined the invitation to view them, and said he would not submit to a reduction in tithes, whereupon Harding remarked that "the farmers have undertaken to raise our wages, and we have undertaken to reduce the tithes."

We assume that the interview ended at this point, for we next hear that at nine o'clock the vicar "saw two flags and a mob of three or four hundred." As well as Aaron Harding he also mentions by name John Cobb who, he says, "was very drunk and took a very violent part," and Robert Holdaway of whom we will hear much more later. They repeated to him their object of raising wages and reducing tithes, then Harding said, "We shall go now and turn out old Harrison first, and then come back to you; stop till we come back, or it will be the worse for you." Part of the mob went off down Gracious Street towards the workhouse "blowing a horn," and about fifty to one hundred others remained near his house, "so that they could watch my motions," as Cobbold later testified.

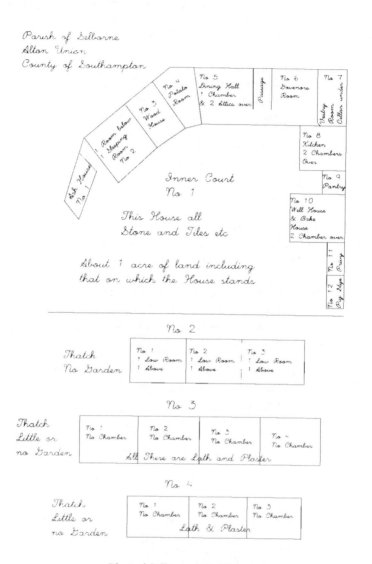

Parish of Selborne
Alton Union
County of Southampton

No 4 Potato Room

No 5 Dining Hall 1 Chamber & 2 Attics over

Passage

No 6 Govenors Room

No 7

No 3 Wood House

Vestry Room Cellar under

Room below Sleeping Room No 2

No 8 Kitchen 2 Chambers Over

Ash House No 1

No 9 Pantry

Inner Court
No 1

No 10 Well House & Bake House 2 Chamber over

This House all
Stone and Tiles etc

No 11 Pig Stye Privy

About 1 acre of land including
that on which the House stands

No 12 Pig Stye Privy

No 2

Thatch
No Garden

No 1 1 Low Room 1 Above	No 2 1 Low Room 1 Above	No 3 1 Low Room 1 Above

No 3

Thatch
Little or
no Garden

No 1 No Chamber	No 2 No Chamber	No 3 No Chamber	No 4 No Chamber
All These are Lath and Plaster			

No 4

Thatch
Little or
no Garden

No 1 No Chamber	No 2 No Chamber	No 3 No Chamber
Lath & Plaster		

Plan of Selborne Workhouse
prepared February 1836 in preparation for its sale

26

At the Poor House in Gracious Street

When the mob arrived at the Poor House they found that Mr Harrison was not at home, though his wife and family were. Considering the fact that he must have been aware something was going on, indeed Bridger claims that the farmers had warned him the evening before, we may find this strange; perhaps he had gone to seek help, perhaps away on unavoidable business— we do not know. The mob "gave the mistress of the house notice to quit before night," but she seems not unnaturally to have taken fright and left the house with her family almost immediately, some say through a back window.

Edward Ticknell recollected later in court how, on hearing that there was trouble, he had gone to the workhouse and found the mob there "pulling tiles off the roof, breaking up furniture and smashing windows." A fire had been started and he saw Bennett throwing water on it. "Newland was there, blowing his horn and carrying the flags," he said, and in less than 15 minutes the house was unroofed, the doors, crockery and windows broken, feather beds pulled to pieces, the furniture destroyed and burnt, and Harrison's grandfather clock thrown on the fire.

Mrs Cowburn mentions fires being started in several places, and that "young Debenham, having attempted to put them out, was almost demolished by the mob." Holdaway also, as related by his counsel later, was "actively engaged in putting out the fire which threatened the destruction of the building."

However, the judge at the subsequent trial observed that "if the destruction of the workhouse had been intended, the fire would probably have been lit in the middle of the room, and not in the chimney as was the case," and guided the jury to declare that "the mob had only intended the destruction of part of the property, and not the whole." They therefore found all the accused 'not guilty,' but the same prisoners were remanded to be indicted later for mobbing the vicar.

Later in the day, Bridger reports that Mr Debenham Snr arrived at Selborne and remonstrated with the mob on its being an "unlawful proceeding," but they immediately surrounded him with uplifted clubs and demanded to know what he meant. This, "with the treatment his son had received at the workhouse before," was enough to convince him that persuasion and not force would be the best option, as they were only a few unarmed men against three hundred.

The Same Day, at Liphook and Steep

Apparently Mrs Harrison fled with her family to Liphook, for we see in a letter written by Henry Budd JP to John Bonham-Carter the next day: "Yesterday they burnt the Poor House at Selborne with all poor Harrison's furniture and wearing apparel, and threatened to murder his family, which Mrs Dowling at the *Anchor* at Liphook has informed me are in her house, and it is said that the people mean to come over tomorrow and have them or destroy the house." He goes on to say that he had stationed soldiers there for their protection, and asks for reinforcements as speedily as possible. More evidence, if any were necessary, of the depth of hatred the people of Selborne felt towards their *Werk'us*, its Master and his family.

The Anchor, Liphook in the mid 1800s

On the same day that Selborne was rioting, Liphook saw a disturbance of its own, at about two o'clock in the afternoon, when a "large and tumultuous assemblage" of 200 to 300 labourers met outside the *Anchor* to complain of low wages. The local men were apparently being incited by a person who was a stranger to the area. Mr Budd and other local landowners were there, trying to persuade them to disperse, when the Regulator coach arrived from London with Dr Quarrier, a magistrate from Steep, inside. He apparently sized up the situation, grabbed the stranger by the collar and, with the help of two constables, bundled him into the coach and sped off with him towards Petersfield, where he was committed and sent on to the Gosport Bridewell. We are told that the Liphook mob then dispersed with no further trouble.

This same Dr Quarrier arrived home at Steep in the evening to consult with John Coles, another of the county's magistrates, and John Bonham-Carter, who was High Sheriff of Hampshire and also MP for Portsmouth, about a meeting of labourers organised by a self-styled 'General Committee' to take place the next day in Steep churchyard. They agreed to send round a request to all the farmers asking them not to allow their labourers to attend the meeting, and this measure succeeded in preventing both the Steep meeting and a subsequent one planned for Wednesday, which was market day, in Petersfield.

But no such remedial action occurred in Selborne or Headley.

Back Outside the Selborne Vicarage

Cobbold had been "expostulating for three quarters of an hour" with that part of the mob left outside his house when he "heard something and went towards the workhouse, and met some persons running in great fear" who warned him to "take care of himself, as the mob were coming back and bent on mischief."

Here we may imagine the somewhat amusing spectacle of the snobbish Rev Cobbold running quickly back to his house, where he waited until the mob returned to The Plestor. He again names Cobb, Trimming and Harding as those pressing against his gate, and he asked them what their object was. Cobb, who was probably still not sober, told him he must lower his tithes to £300 a year, and Harding "repeated the same in a very violent manner." Cobbold says he told them "they could not be in earnest." According to Cowburn, the mob, now swollen in number to over 400, gave Cobbold half an hour to make a decision, and "when that time had expired, just 5 minutes more," before "a rush was about to take place upon him and his house."

Apparently Holdaway was prominent in holding back the mob, and particularly Cobb, at this juncture. Bridger claims it was the farmers who asked him to do it, but Holdaway had his own reasons for being there. Cobbold had persevered for years to have Holdaway expelled from *The Compasses*, the only Public House in Selborne at the time, where he had been landlord. Cowburn writes: "I will not say Holdaway did not keep an irregular house, but I will say that, in my opinion, it was not worse than at neighbouring places." Cobbold had eventually succeeded in having him expelled, and Holdaway had been unemployed since. During the arguments that arose during the expulsion, it seems that Cobbold told Holdaway he would show him "no mercy." Holdaway was now able to turn the tables and embarrass the clergyman with a display of Christian charity, saying to him: "Now, sir, you once told me you would have no mercy on me—you see I have had mercy on you."

And here for the first time we see the direct involvement, or rather non-involvement, of the farmers. Cobbold says that several farmers (some reports say ten) were present, but they "merely looked on tamely." He claimed that one of them, who was High Constable, said it was no use to resist such a mob, and another, Hori Hale, said, 'For God's sake accept of £300 a year; if you don't you'll be murdered and your house pulled down.' Seeing such lack of support by those from whom he might reasonably have expected more, he "found it necessary to submit," adding that nothing but a firm conviction that he "should otherwise be destroyed" induced him to do so.

Mr Hale communicated to the mob that the vicar had agreed, at which they cheered and asked "to have it in black and white." Cobbold then sent Henry Eade, a churchwarden, into the house to draw up an agreement, and when it was brought out he signed it. The mob called for the farmers to witness it, which they did with a show of reluctance in some cases, and, when the contents of the paper had been read out, asked for a copy of it which Henry Eade duly went back into the house to make. The original was given by Mr H Cole, the vicar's bailiff, to farmer Bridger, and the copy given to a representative of the mob.

The mob then called for £5 for beer, which Cobbold says he "told them they should not have." He claims the farmers let him down again, for he says that "one of the principal farmers proposed that I should let them have £2 worth of beer, and put it down in the poor-book. I said, 'Do as you like.'" But Bridger's version of events is rather different, as he says that Cobbold "was the first to propose its being charged to the Parish account, and mentioned how much he thought each man should have." He also says that Henry Eade "wished half the beer to be had from his house," though he does not mention which house this might be. The farmers, he says, had "refused for some time to give any beer, and only consented at last on condition they (the mob) should immediately disperse and go to their work."

Whoever suggested it, the beer was ordered by the farmers from a public house, presumably *The Compasses*, and brought out in buckets to the men; and the bill which came to £3 17s was duly charged to the Poor Rate. Then the mob dispersed, having remained outside the vicarage and "conducted themselves in a particularly violent manner" for three hours according to Cobbold. The farmers, strongly admonished later by the trial judge for their inaction, pleaded that they were forced to attend. We may rather think that they were there to ensure they got what they wanted out of the day's proceedings.

Cowburn says that the remainder of that night was passed by the mob in "eating, drinking and rioting." His wife wrote letters to him (for he was not himself in Selborne on this day) in which she says that the mob had stopped the Gosport Coach and one other carriage during the day and made them give money, but that she and her family were not troubled, even though they were "almost the only assailable family" in Selborne. Cowburn himself puts this down to his efforts, over the 8 or 9 years he had been living there, in being "attentive" to the poor of the parish, and giving "any poor man who desired it an acre or two each, to enable them to grow their own potatoes and wheat for bread." He records that when his manservant asked the mob collected at his gate what they wanted, they replied: "Nothing here; this gentleman and lady bear too good characters and are too good to the poor, and we will not hurt a stick or stone about them."

Holdaway and Newland

Two names which, for most people, are synonymous with the Selborne riot are those of Robert Holdaway and John Newland, the Ringleader and the 'Trumpeter' respectively. We have mentioned their names already, but it seems that both of their roles at Selborne may have been less than the popular legends would have us believe.

Robert Holdaway (40) is described as a carpenter, wheelwright, hop planter and former landlord of *The Compasses* (renamed the *Queens Inn* in 1839). Although sometimes referred to as a widower, he was at the time of the riot married to his second wife Sarah Freeman, daughter of a big butcher in Alresford, by whom he had five children then aged between one and eight. He also had two children aged 17 and 14 by a previous marriage to Elizabeth Mayhew. According to his children's baptism records, he appears to have moved to Selborne from the Alresford area in 1822/23, but we shall see later that he was also known in Headley and it seems likely that he was a relatively well travelled man around the locality. He was, as stated by Cowburn, currently unemployed due to his previous altercations with Cobbold.

Records of the time say that he was "chosen by the mob to take the agreement round to the neighbouring farmers to get them to sign it as well. This he agreed to do." The choice of Holdaway was approved by the farmers present, and his counsel later made the point that this was perhaps "because he was a man of more discretion than the rest." Apparently the signatures of several individuals in the Newton Valence and Hartley Mauditt areas were obtained later that same day, and Holdaway had proposed to proceed alone with the agreement to other places the next day, but "the mob would not hear of this and insisted they would accompany him." It would appear that he was at best a reluctant hero. At his trial, Harriet Freeman (his sister-in-law) stated that she was at his house when the mob called on the Monday and forced him away, and he himself also stated at his trial that all he did was to "go about with the mob to prevent them from doing any mischief."

As a footnote, it is interesting to note vicar Cobbold's subsequent statements about Holdaway. At the trial, he said he had known Holdaway for 8 years, that he was of Selborne parish, and he would "rather not be asked" as to his character; but he also "begged to state, as an act of justice to Holdaway, that he saved his (Cobbold's) life and property on the 22nd by his influence over the mob that were about his house." Later, in March 1832, when a petition seems to have been raised on Holdaway's behalf for his return, Cobbold wrote of him as being "of notorious memory on account of the leading part he took in the riots of this neighbourhood." He obviously did not want to see him back in Selborne.

John Newland (39) was, "like all the Newlands," according to a grand-daughter of his, "a big strong man." He had seen service in the North Hampshire Regiment, and had collected a wound in the head while on service abroad which meant that even a small amount of drink affected him. He lived in a cottage in Adams Lane with his wife Ann and, in 1830, eight children (two by Ann's previous marriage) ranging in age from 12 years to six months. Records show the family receiving 11/6d a week from the Poor Rate in October 1827, made up of 8/- for his wife and his children, 2/6d for his wife's children and 1/- for an 'ill child'. He is described as a farm labourer, and at his trial was given a good character reference both by farmer Edward Fitt and by Cobbold himself, who said he was a quiet, inoffensive man, except when he had been drinking.

Legend says that he led the Selborne rioters and rallied them with his horn, but in his testimony at the trial he claims that he was pressed by Aaron Harding to leave his work on the Monday and go with them, that he blew his horn only once at the desire of some of the men, and that in the evening he was "knocked down by some of the party for not having taken an active part at the workhouse." He also implies that he followed the mob to Headley on the following day, but we hear no mention of him there. A warrant for his arrest was issued the following Monday for his part in the Selborne events.

There is a further popular legend that he escaped arrest by hiding in the woods above the village, coming down to his cottage at night for food. He may have evaded capture for a while by this means, but it would be for two nights at the most, since his testimony states that he "went to work and was taken on the Friday" following the riot, which would make him one of the earlier men to be picked up. It is interesting to note that one of the names on his warrant is E. Knight Jnr—could it be that, along with his other claims to fame, Newland was also arrested by Jane Austen's nephew?

Others arrested for the Selborne riot were: John Trimming (25), John Cobb (27), Benjamin Smith (23), William Bicknell (23), Thomas Hoare (36), William Hoare (39), Henry Bone (31), and Robert Bennett (16) — all labourers we think. Aaron Harding and Robert Holdaway were charged instead with the events at Headley, which were regarded as more serious offences.

Robert Holdaway's signature in Selborne vestry minutes of 11th April 1823

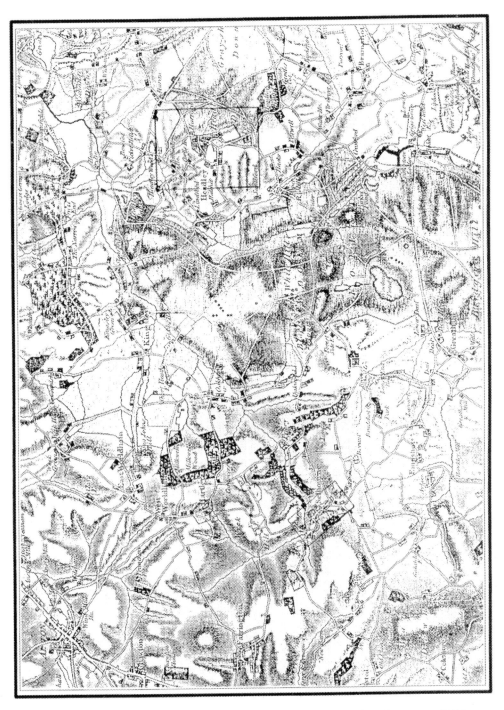

Alton – Liphook area: from 1" Ordnance Survey maps dated prior to 1815

To Headley and Kingsley
Tuesday 23rd November 1830

Why Headley?

We must now ask ourselves why the Selborne mob should, after they had seemingly achieved their own parochial ends, march some seven miles on a cold November day to Headley, in a neighbouring parish, to repeat the same procedure there.

Given that the population of adult males (over 20 years old) in Selborne was just under 200 at the time, some of the estimated 300 or more rioters present on the Monday must have come from outside the parish, as indeed contemporary reports imply. It may be that these included 'helpers' from Headley who came on a mutual understanding that assistance would be returned in kind on the following day—but this is pure conjecture on our part.

Mrs Cowburn also tells her husband on Monday evening that the Selborne men were going tomorrow "to demolish the workhouse at Headleigh *(sic)* where young Harrison is." She does not make it clear whether she is referring to the master of Selborne workhouse or a son of his, or in what capacity he was there, and Headley records do not mention him, but it leaves the possibility that the move to Headley was in part at least a continuation of the Selborne vendetta against the Harrisons.

What we do know is that people in Headley were aware in advance that trouble was heading their way. At 8 o'clock on Tuesday morning Matthew Triggs and his brother William went to Headley Poor House to try to fetch out their uncle, a pauper named Tuckey, and take him down to their sisters, because they said they thought "there would be a row or a piece of work at the house that day." Mr James Shoesmith, the Master of Headley Poor House, refused to let him go saying, "No, I can't spare him, for if there is to be a row he can speak more and better to the purpose than any person else." He gave the Triggs brothers a pint of beer each and they went away—but Matthew was to return later.

In the meantime, the Selborne mob had "called on Robert Holdaway again this morning and pressed him to go with them to gather more signatures on their agreement." Apparently there were rumours that there was to be another attack made on Cobbold, but "this proved untrue and only about 60 Selborne and Oakhanger men came here this morning," according to Mrs Cowburn in Selborne. Her husband reports that on that morning "the banner was again displayed, their force called together by the sound of horns and, compelling all labourers everywhere to join, they accumulated it is said 1,100 and proceeded to Headley."

In fact there is reason to believe that this figure relates to their number by the time they had arrived at Headley, and that considerably fewer started from Selborne; but whatever the number, Selborne was very empty that day. The leaders of the mob appear to have pressed all the men in the village to their cause, with "threats used to those who deserted." Mrs Cowburn, in a letter written the following day, says "there was scarcely a man in the place," and describes how "the silence throughout the village, with here and there a woman or a child straggling about, was quite awful, and all sorts of reports were in circulation as to what was going on." She also said that the children would never forget 'the mob'—"they thought it fun at first, but then got rather frightened."

The mob went first to farms in the Empshott and Greatham area, and Cowburn says that at Empshott, Holdaway "stayed the fury of the worst man in the parish when directed against the chief farmer." From Greatham they set out for Headley where a meeting had been called by the farmers and the clergy there to discuss the issue of labourers wages. It was to take place at the *Bush Inn* (the *Holly Bush*). From this we deduce that the overt purpose of Holdaway's journey to Headley was to attend the prearranged meeting but, as we have said, the mob accompanying him were also expected and the threat to Headley Poor House known about, at least to some in the village. Certainly Mr Bennett, a farmer of Hilland in Headley, had moved his threshing machine out of the way (as he thought) to Kingsley in anticipation of trouble.

On the March

Whatever its motive, the circuitous march from Selborne to Headley began early on Tuesday morning. One farmer's labourer stated later that "a mob had come to him the preceding day and he went with them at six the next morning towards Headley ... a distance of more than six miles." He claimed (before a magistrate the next day) that he went with the mob "by desire of his master, he (the master) being threatened." Before the mob arrived at Headley he said "they went to several farm houses and other places" and he saw money collected. There is also reason to believe that men were pressed into joining the mob at each house visited. We are told that Holdaway was carrying a paper "obviously written by a man of education," which we assume was the farmers' agreement to raise wages on which he was collecting signatures.

By the time they arrived at Standford there were already many hundreds of marchers present and here, we are told, they were joined by "forest dwellers and travellers," swelling their numbers even further. Estimates vary between several hundred and more than a thousand, but it is certain that the mob which marched up Tulls Lane and along Liphook Road into Headley was significantly larger than that which had been seen in Selborne the previous day.

One resident of Standford was Mr Curtis, a shopkeeper in Headley. His house, now called *Wood House*, overlooks Standford Green and he would have had a good view of the mob there if he was at home. One unconfirmed report hints that he may have been sworn in at Liphook that day by Henry Budd as a special constable to read the Riot Act at Headley, but we have found no corroboration of this, and certainly the Riot Act was not mentioned at the subsequent trials.

As an aside, a further report which is often quoted, telling of the mob talking to a Mr Curtis later about their endeavours ("Oh Mr Curtis, it is a pity you were not at Headley ..."), refers to Mr Curtis of Alton, who met stragglers going home up East Worldham hill at the end of the day, not to Mr Curtis of Standford and Headley. We shall refer to Mr Curtis of Alton again later.

Meanwhile in Headley

While the Selborne mob was travelling towards its destination, growing all the time, things were happening in Headley itself. We have already mentioned the visit of the Triggs brothers to the Poor House first thing in the morning. Following that, Matthew Triggs seems to have been active in raising a local Headley mob which went round the village pressing more men to join in, and demanding money and food from shopkeepers and householders.

Matthew (38), of Hollywater in Headley parish, is described as having been a bricklayer for 20 years. He was married to Mary Croucher and they had five children aged between 9 years and six months. At the time he appears to have been employed helping to refurbish the Rectory, which still stands in Headley High Street. It must have been a fairly substantial job of work, because the Rector and his family had moved out while it was going on and were staying with the Bennetts at Hilland Farm.

At Headley Rectory

One of the workmen at the Rectory, Mr Tend, was a painter and paper-hanger of Kennington, London, and he appears to have brought a number of other London workmen with him. According to him, when they were in the kitchen that morning "some men came to us, Matthew Triggs and his brother were there, and they told us that I and my friends must go with them to Headley Green. I said that I would not go on any consideration and nor should any of my men. They said if we did not go they would force us."

Headley Rectory in the 1800s

Triggs and the others retired, presumably for consultation, then came back in greater numbers. They first said very civilly, "Gentlemen, you must come with us," but when Mr Tend again refused they threatened to set fire to the Rectory and to murder him and his men. "They had all of them famous large bludgeons of tremendous size," he commented later. At this he begged for half an hour to consider matters, which they granted, but when he attempted to go out to consult the rector, who as we have said was living in a different part of the village at the time, the mob surrounded him and threatened again to take his life if he tried to escape them. "I did not go after all," he said. But he did see Matthew Triggs and the mob attempt to take away Triggs' master by force, and later when Triggs was the only Headley man convicted for the events which occurred in the village that day, it was due largely it seems to the testimony of Mr Tend against him.

Mobbing the Headley Rector

Precisely what happened in Headley before the larger Selborne mob arrived is not quite clear. Speaking more than forty years after the event, John Lickfold, a shopkeeper at the time, is reported to have told how he gave some men "seven loaves and some cheese" and then, with the aid of a friend, drove them out of his shop. He said the mob went round begging all they could, and when he saw them coming back later he put his loaded gun out on the counter to make sure he was paid for the "ounce of baccy" they wanted this time.

At about ten o'clock, Mr Shoesmith walked from the Poor House along to the Village Green and saw "a mob of about 200 or 250 persons assembled, and others kept coming up." He identified James Painter, a 36 year old labourer from Kingsley, who was married with a one year old daughter and was later to be arrested for riot, as being there on the Green, and he also saw the rector, Rev Robert Dickinson, "coming out of a garden and followed by a part of the mob." It seems that the rector had got wind of trouble and had gone down the road to see Mr Ewsters at Arford House. But the local mob found out where he was and, in Mr Lickfold's words, "they dragged him out, and his wife too, Mrs Dickinson, and they brought them all up the Green, and the women patted them on the back saying, 'Aha! you'll come down three hundred I know,' and they made him sign a paper that he wouldn't take more than so much tithe." Mr Dickinson is reported to have agreed to reduce his tithes to £350 a year (the Clergy List for 1842 states the tithe value for Headley as £726). We are not sure who led this group since, unlike the mobbing of Cobbold in Selborne, no charges were ever brought against those mobbing Dickinson, and therefore we have no evidence from a trial.

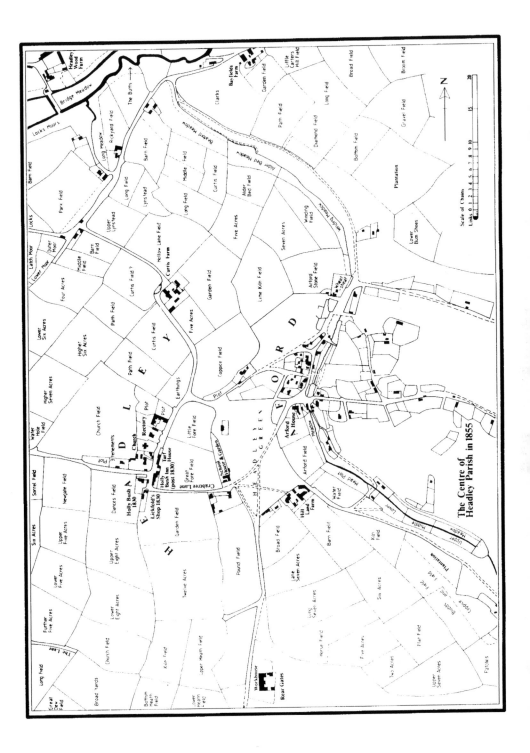

The Centre of
Headley Parish in 1855

The Selborne Mob Arrives

Mr Shoesmith returned to the Poor House, and in about a quarter of an hour some local people warned him that a mob was coming. This was not the Headley mob which he had just seen on the Village Green, but the Selborne mob coming from the opposite direction. Mr Lickfold claims he had gone down to the Poor House at Mr Shoesmith's request, and the two of them supply us with eye-witness accounts of what happened next. By Lickfold's estimate there were two to three hundred men coming up the road, by Shoesmith's there were upwards of a thousand and "they all had sticks." They also had a kind of a red, or a red, white and yellow flag on a pole, according to a Headley farmer Eli Smith, who was with them. Robert Holdaway appears to have been at the head of them, and we are given the impression of him halting his mob outside the gates of the Poor House and going up to the door to see Shoesmith. The latter obviously knew him, for he allegedly greeted him with the words, "What Holdy, are you here?" whereupon Holdaway is said to have replied, "Yes, but I mean you no harm, nor your wife, nor your goods, so get them out as soon as you can, for the house must come down."

Shoesmith replied that they had "a number of old persons in the house and some children ill with a fever," and Holdaway said they would be protected and taken care of if the window where they were was marked. Shoesmith then tried to argue his case saying, "If any person can say I have acted unfairly by any poor man, let it be revenged on me, not on the house," and Eli Smith confirmed later that he himself had "never heard any complaint of ill-treatment of any of the paupers in Headley Workhouse." Smith claimed that he was only there because he had been pressed to do so, and said to Shoesmith, "I have done all in my power to try to dissuade them from doing this, but I have not succeeded."

At this point Lickfold recalls that Shoesmith asked for time "to take out our traps," and Holdaway agreed to give him two hours. Some of the mob apparently rushed towards the house then, but were quickly called back by Henry James, a 38 year old widower with 7 children, nearly six foot in height and described variously as a gypsy brazier, tinman, knife-grinder and soldier. We are unclear where he came from; he may have been one of the "forest dwellers and travellers" who joined the mob as it passed through Standford, but we do know that Shoesmith says he was "not from Headley." He seems to have had a commanding presence, for he apparently shut the gate and told the mob, "No-one shall enter here at present." He then volunteered to help Shoesmith remove his goods from the house while Holdaway led the rest of the mob off towards the Village Green, but he may have had less than honourable motives in doing this, as we hear later of his "large family" taking away some of the property belonging to the Poor House and selling it. Shoesmith nevertheless thanked him for his help at the time.

The Meeting in the 'Holly Bush'

It is generally assumed that the two mobs now met up on Headley Green for the first time but, since the Poor House is less than half a mile away down a fairly straight road, it is far more likely that the Headley mob had already heard the others coming and had run down to see what was going on. The general character of the meeting was described as "riotous and tumultuous," and one person estimated 1,700 to 1,800 people to be present at this point.

We understand that Holdaway met the Rector of Headley on the Green as the latter "came by on his way to *The Bush*," and was asked by him to come to the meeting and bring the agreement along. The mob followed them up Crabtree Lane, and Holdaway and Mr Dickinson "went into *The Bush* to join the farmers already assembled there."

After some discussion, the meeting agreed that tithes would be reduced and labourers wages increased; we are not told by how much, nor whether it only affected Headley. The farmers then all made a small contribution, amounting to some £7, to be shared out among the labourers, and Holdaway left the meeting to pass on the news to the people waiting outside. After reading out the agreement and telling them how much money the farmers had contributed, he learned that while he had been inside the pub some of the mob had returned to the Poor House and had begun to demolish it. When the farmers heard this they asked Holdaway to go and use what influence he had to stop the destruction.

Holdaway tried to enlist the help of the local people, asking "all you Headley people" to go with him to the Poor House. This phrase was later used in evidence against him at the trial by one Richard Rook, a local labourer, who implied that by using it, Holdaway was inciting the Headley people to join in the destruction. Holdaway's counsel was to describe Rook as "a man of infamous character" who, after Holdaway's conviction, "indecently boasted that he had 'Done the B....r.'"

Other more reputable witnesses, who were not called at the trial, asserted that Holdaway "exerted himself continually in endeavouring upon different parts of the mob not to go to the Poor House"; that he "begged and prayed—begged and entreated that the mob would do no injury to it"; that he "stood still to do so—and this not once only but several times," reasoning with them "upon the folly and ingratitude of their conduct." But all his entreaties were to no avail; as another witness testified, "the Headley men were so resolute and determined, that he could not keep them back," and he set off for the Poor House followed by many of the local labourers who, it seemed, were determined to join in the fray.

Sacking of Headley Poor House

Shoesmith says he had removed most of his goods by the time the mob came back at around midday having been away for about an hour. He described how he was upstairs with his wife in the room where the sick children were when "the mob rushed like a torrent into every room and began breaking the windows and partitions." Mrs Shoesmith spoke to Henry James and begged him to put somebody at the door to protect the room. He did this, and then assisted her downstairs to the yard. Mrs Cowburn, writing from Selborne the next day, reports hearing a rumour that "they brought out two poor women ill with a fever and one poor child dead from the workhouse before they began their work."

The destruction was already well under way when Holdaway reached the house, and although he reportedly kept calling to the men, "Come away, we have done enough," they took no notice of him and carried on sacking the building for an hour to an hour and a half. Shoesmith mentions seeing James Painter breaking the banisters of the staircase while the rest of the mob were breaking up doors, tearing out windows and taking down the ceilings. Mr Lickfold talks of seeing them putting their sticks through the roof "till the dust looked like smoke." After that they made their way through the roof and began to remove the tiles, stripping some 40,000 to 50,000 off in all. Shoesmith particularly noticed that Matthew Triggs, the bricklayer who had come for his uncle that morning, was on the roof at this time.

Some of the mob took a 40 gallon copper out of the brickwork and rolled it into the yard and began to beat on it with their bludgeons, others found 30 gallons of Shoesmith's home-made wine in the cellar and started to drink it. He recorded that, "Aaron Harding was doing nothing but drinking my wine; James Painter was astride on my cask; there were many men and women drinking it out of tins and other vessels about the yard; Thomas Harding was there and he was quite drunk." Thomas, a 32 year old bachelor and a farm labourer from Kingsley, was Aaron's younger brother.

Some women were obviously involved in the rioting along with the men. We heard earlier how women were patting the rector on the back when he was mobbed on the Green, and here we are told of some drinking Shoesmith's wine. Lickfold also talks of women carrying off all the bedding and blankets from the sacked house. Altogether it was estimated that about £200 worth of blankets and other property was taken away, and "very little of it was returned," according to Mr Sparrow, one of the Poor House Visitors from Bramshott.

At the end it was reported that "there was not one room left entire, except that in which the sick children were." An estimated £1,000 worth of damage had been done, and when Robert Holdaway was asked what he thought of the work he replied, "I am sorry to see it—it is too bad—it will hang me."

At Last to Kingsley

After much persuasion, Holdaway at last managed to draw many of the mob off with him towards Kingsley, three miles away, where he encouraged several more farmers to sign the agreement. However, as we mentioned earlier, it was also to Kingsley that Mr Bennett had moved his threshing machine from Headley for safety and, whether by design or by chance, the mob seems to have taken the opportunity to find it and break it while they were there. As far as we know, this, along with another example in Wyck the next day, was one of very few examples of machine breaking to occur in the local parishes, although machinery was a favourite target for rioters elsewhere in Hampshire and southern England.

A horse-driven threshing machine circa 1830

We are not sure what size the mob was by the time it reached Kingsley, but we know it contained representatives from 10 parishes, which we assume were: Selborne, Headley, Bramshott, Kingsley, East Worldham, West Worldham, Hartley Mauditt, Newton Valence, Empshott, and Greatham. Here "on Kingsley Green," according to the judge speaking to Holdaway at his trial, you "called out ten persons as the representatives of the ten parishes of which the labourers had formed your dangerous and illegal assembly, in order that you might reward them for their iniquity, and divided the forced contributions collected in the course of the day, and which did not amount to less than £23, among them." According to Mrs Cowburn, speaking of her experience in Selborne that evening, all of this money "went I fear at the public houses, and it ended, as such things do, in fighting."

Where Next?

There is evidence to suggest that the mob wanted to go on to Alton the next day and sack the 'Union' Poor House and the breweries there. Mrs Cowburn writes on this day that she had heard "there is likely to be a great disturbance at Alton; they expect fourteen or fifteen hundred there." Holdaway refused to go with them, after the experience at Headley, and in the event Alton was not disturbed. This may have been due to a loss of momentum when the mob dispersed at Kingsley that night, or because they guessed at the more determined defence which Alton was preparing to put up to counter any attack. We assume the members of the mob went from Kingsley back to their ten parishes, but there is reason to suspect that some stayed on to cause trouble locally. Certainly John Kingshott (35), a married farm labourer with 5 children who lived in Greatham, was later arrested for stealing loaves of bread, cheese and beer from Mary King in Kingsley that day, along with Thomas Marshall (21) who was also charged with demolishing Headley Poor House.

As for John Newland, the Trumpeter of Selborne, he claimed he had been "so much in liquor" on Monday night that he had slept in the fields all that night, and the next morning went down "all wet and chilled" to the public house where he got some more beer. This affected his head so much that he remained all day Tuesday with the mob "without knowing what he was about." He had no recollection of anything till he found himself ill in bed in his own house the following day.

Some of the mob, returning up East Worldham Hill, met Mr Curtis of Alton (previously mentioned) riding on one of his rounds on his way to Kingsley. He recalls the "large crowd of excited rioters" said to him: "'Oh Mr Curtis, it is a pity you were not at Headley when we broke into the workhouse. You would have laughed if you had seen the tiles fly. Tell the people of Alton to look out as we are intending to attack the Workhouse and Breweries.'" On his return home he made known what he had seen and heard, and a messenger was sent on horseback to Winchester for troops, and a number of the inhabitants were sworn in as special constables; the town was patrolled at night, and "every precaution taken against an attack." The guard room was an old hop store used by Messrs Crowley, and situated at the corner of Turk Street. Mrs Cowburn heard from the Clerk at Selborne that they "are prepared for them at Alton and determined to resist them; 140 constables are sworn in."

Wednesday 24th November 1830

James John Hugonin, an Alton magistrate and ex-military man, writing to John Bonham-Carter on the following day, said that he was "happy to inform" that the "determined threats of the mob to pull down our Poor House have not been attempted." He added that he had been in "no apprehension" of his own parish doing anything, but "the mob from the lawless districts of Selborne, Kingsley, Hawkley, etc is of a more formidable description than the common run of mobs at present." He said that he had 30 soldiers with which he could "prevent any violence by any number of the mob," and adds, "you will probably think that this smacks too much of the old Soldier."

At Selborne, Mrs Cowburn reported that "all here seems to wear a peaceful aspect this morning and the men have returned to their work" and that "it is quite delightful to hear the sound of the flail." Many farmers had sat up all the previous night in case of trouble, but now many of the rioters "have had quite enough of their two days." Her labourer Thomas, who had been pressed to go along with the rest, told her it had been "very hungry work—he got nothing; the first got what was to be had, and those behind were obliged to go without." She also says that a few men came over from Worldham on Wednesday morning to ask for help, but were told "no," the Selborne men "had done with it and they must fight their own battles," and that these Worldham men had not come to help them in Selborne earlier in the week. *(See facsimile on next page)*

Whether or not it relates to the same men we do not know, but one more event did occur on that day. At Wyck, between East Worldham and Binsted, a mob including some men from Selborne parish attempted to break a threshing machine "of the value of twenty-five pounds" belonging to Robert Shotter and Edward Baigent. For this the brothers William and Thomas Heighes of Shortheath were later arrested and, while William (30) was acquitted with a severe caution, Thomas (28), married to Ann (née Bright) and with two children aged three and one year old, gained the unenviable distinction of being the first of the local men to be transported for one of the last acts they committed.

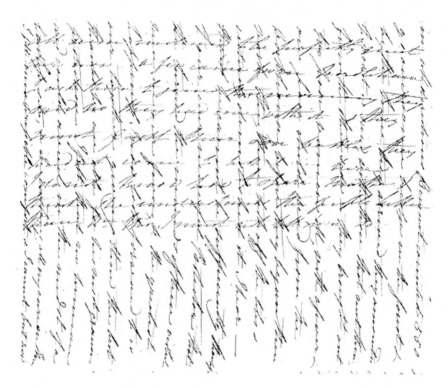

"*All seem inclined to be perfectly quiet here now. A few came from Worldham to ask them to join this morning. They said, no they must fight their own battles. They had not come to help them here.*" – Part of Mrs Cowburn's letter to her husband written on Wednesday 24th November, 1830.

The Round Up: Thursday 25th November to Wednesday 15th December, 1830

The Gentry form 'Snatch Squads'

We know that a few soldiers were stationed at Alton and at Liphook during, or soon after, the Selborne and Headley disturbances, but they seem to have been used largely to deter rioters from going to those places. According to John Lickfold, some 15 to 20 mounted soldiers rode into Headley about two days after the disturbances there, and we also have an account by Ann Shrubb who was six years old at the time, telling how she saw the soldiers through their schoolroom window—and that their master, Mr Allfield, pulled down the blind to stop them looking. But it appears that the soldiers did little more than just pass through.

If these were the same Dragoons as those reported to have been billeted at the *Anchor* in Liphook, they could well have been preoccupied with other problems. We are told that while the landlady, Mrs Dowling, was asleep they had broken into her liquor stores, and drunk so much gin that stomach pumps had to be used to save their lives.

The rounding up of known rioters was left to local magistrates, assisted by bailiffs and other helpers, and with the military sometimes in attendance. We hear of Henry Budd JP, a Deputy Lieutenant of Hampshire who lived at Foley near Liphook, and Rev John Coles JP who is believed to have come from Buriton, riding out all day with parties of men and bringing in suspects to Liphook. Cowburn himself says he aided Budd, "assisted as he was by a detachment of Dragoons," to take Holdaway.

Hugonin, Edward Knight Jnr and other magistrates from Alton were likewise involved. The vicar of Empshott, Mr Charles Alcock, states in a letter to Cowburn that Guards were used to take Newland, and we assume these were from the troop of Life Guards quartered in the *Crown Inn* at Alton, as mentioned by J. Curtis in his 1896 publication: *A Short History of Alton*.

Mr Alcock also observes, on Sunday 28th November, that "almost all Greatham labourers are in custody," and says that Kingshott, in particular, "made great resistance and attempted the life of young Debenham."

Remembering his treatment by the mob at Selborne workhouse, poor Debenham Jnr seems to have been in the wars, all in all. Alcock notes that he saw him on horseback "with a gun, guarding a cart of prisoners." One may imagine how relieved he must have felt to have got them safely in custody at last.

John Bonham-Carter came up to Liphook from Petersfield to help with the committals, and in letters between Budd and himself and between himself and his wife, we are given a feel for the way in which the operation was handled.

On Thursday 25th November, two days after the Headley riot, Budd writes to say that they had taken Robert Holdaway, Aaron Harding and John Cobb, all of Selborne, plus one Harding of Kingsley, and that Matthew Triggs of Headley—"a very bad case"—was also in custody. He explains that he had just returned home having been out since 9 o'clock in the morning, and that his hands were so cold he had to ask his wife to write the letter for him. He states that Coles had sent in seven others, and was currently still out at Empshott taking one more. Coles returned at half past seven in the evening, in time to add a postscript to Budd's letter confirming his success in taking the man, and saying that this made a total of 13 in all.

Fire in Selborne

However, this did not mean that all was peace and quiet. Alcock, in his letter to Cowburn on 28th November, is "horror struck" to learn, as he came out of church that day, that there had been a serious fire in Selborne. He fears in case it was wilfully started, and Curtis in his *Short History of Alton* mentions that the Life Guards went once more to Selborne "when rioters set fire to a public house." It must have been *The Compasses*, since Cowburn tells us that this was the only public house in Selborne at the time, but we can only guess as to the reason for the arson.

By Fish Cart from Liphook

On or about Saturday 4th December, John Bonham-Carter went to Liphook early in the morning to confront the prisoners and assist in making out committals there, and returned "in the rear of 12 prisoners chained together in a fish cart." In a letter to his wife he makes a point of stressing that they were escorted under the civil power of 6 constables, rather than by soldiers. We assume that they were taken to Gosport Bridewell and held there until they could be accommodated at Winchester, for we hear of Coles riding with them as far as Horndean. We know on the evidence of his counsel that Holdaway, for example, did not arrive in Winchester until 3 days before his trial.

It is likely that the prisoners committed by Hugonin and other magistrates from Alton were taken directly to Winchester. Altogether we know of 22 local men who were committed for acts relating to the activities of the Selborne and Headley mobs, out of a total of 345 arrested for disturbances in Hampshire as a whole at this time.

The Trials
Monday 20th to Thursday 30th December

The Special Commission

Such were the number of cases awaiting trial throughout southern England that the County Gaols were full to overflowing and, rather than try to handle all through the regular local Assizes, the Government appointed Special Commissions to clear the backlog and also to ensure consistent and strict sentencing between different Counties.

The first of these started in Winchester on Monday 20th December and dealt with prisoners arrested in Hampshire. Sir John Vaughan, Baron of the Exchequer, was the chief judge and he was assisted by Sir James Parke and Sir Edward Alderson. The Duke of Wellington, in his capacity as Lord Lieutenant of Hampshire, also sat on the bench. The trials were held in The Castle at Winchester before petty juries selected from a Grand Jury of 23 gentlemen, thirteen of whom were baronets or knights, and lasted, with a break of two days for Christmas, through until Thursday 30th December.

The Selborne Trials

Prisoners were brought to the dock several at a time, and on the morning of Thursday 23rd December we find ten men (Aaron Harding, John Cobb, William Hoare, Thomas Hoare, Henry Bone, John Newland, William Bicknell, Benjamin Smith, Robert Bennett and John Trimming) put to the bar charged with having "along with a large mob, riotously assembled on the 22nd of November in the parish of Selborne, and feloniously and with force begun to demolish the Poor House of the said parish." As we noted earlier, they were found 'not guilty' of this charge on a technicality, but all except Aaron Harding were tried again six days later for having "by threats compelled the Rev William Cobbold to sign a paper agreeing to reduce his tithes to £300," and this time all except Bicknell and Bennett were found 'guilty' and given prison sentences with hard labour.

Harding was not charged again only because he had in the meantime been tried and convicted for the more serious crime of destroying the Poor House at Headley, and we suspect this was also the reason why Robert Holdaway was not charged with any Selborne offences.

During the Selborne trials, farmer Edward Fitt spoke in defence of a number of the labourers, including Newland and Benjamin Smith, and was admonished by the judge, who said he "wished to hold out to the farmers that they were running into great peril in exciting persons to act in such a way," and that he "could not help saying" that he very much regretted not seeing some of them at that bar. Fitt's action also seems to have displeased his fellow farmers, for James Bridger writes later: "I think we should not have had such blame thrown upon us if Ed. Fitt had not given such miserable evidence" in the court.

The Headley Trial

The Headley case was the first to be heard after the Christmas break, on Monday 27th December, when seven men (Robert Holdaway, Matthew Triggs, Henry James, James Painter, John Heath, Aaron Harding and Thomas Harding) were put to the bar charged with having "with divers others, riotously and unlawfully assembled at Headley on the 23rd of November and, when so assembled, feloniously pulled down and demolished the Poor House of the united parishes of Bramshott, Headley and Kingsley." They were also charged with *beginning* to pull it down, which was probably a more accurate description.

Such a felony attracted the death penalty, and in a trial lasting over 8 hours all seven were found guilty. Special mention was made of Holdaway's apparent role as leader of the mob, and when sentences were imposed three days later he was the only one of them who was 'left for execution'; Heath, James, Triggs and Aaron Harding were given terms of transportation for life, and Thomas Harding and James Painter for 7 years. Thomas Robinson (67) and William Bright (22) were both acquitted of offences committed in Headley.

Kingsley and Wyck Trials

Of the other local men arrested in relation to the Selborne/Headley mob, John Kingshott and Thomas Marshall were both sentenced to death for their robbery of loaves, cheese and beer at Kingsley (although Kingshott's conduct record states his offence as "machine breaking") and for Marshall's part in the riot at Headley. Kingshott's sentence was commuted to life transportation, and Marshall's to imprisonment for just one year because of unrecorded "mitigating circumstances."

Thomas Heighes was sentenced to 7 years transportation for damaging the threshing machine at Wyck. It is interesting to note that damaging a threshing machine was not generally regarded as a capital offence, whereas damaging other machinery or buildings or committing a robbery were so regarded in those days.

Reaction to Sentences

Petitions to the Home Office and Reprieves

Transportation was as good as a death sentence to the wives and families left destitute by the removal of their bread-winner, and the *Times* reported from Winchester that "scenes of distress in and about the jail are most terrible," with wives, sisters, mothers and children "besetting the gates every day." The prison governor admitted that the scenes he was obliged to witness at the time of locking up the prison were "truly heart-breaking," and the general harshness of the sentences imposed brought a storm of protest from all classes of society. Petitions were sent to the Home Office from many towns in Hampshire, including one from Winchester signed by "the clergy of the low church, some of the bankers, and every trader in the town without exception."

Partly due to this pressure, four of the six prisoners who had been 'left for execution' were reprieved, including Robert Holdaway, for whom William Cowburn, from his office in London, was very active. In this he had the backing of "almost all the landowners and occupiers in Selborne and its vicinity" in the form of a petition drawn up by Mr Dunn, the under sheriff. At the beginning of January, Cowburn wrote to Baron Vaughan, the Duke of Wellington, Lord Londonderry, the Duke of Rutland and Lord Melbourne (the Home Secretary) among others, putting the case for commuting Holdaway's sentence to one of life transportation.

"I would not take away life, but banish them, they are not worthy to live in England," he writes of the rioters in a letter to Lord Londonderry. To Vaughan he says, "I venture to say the punishment of death on Holdaway will do harm in Selborne and Headley; a feeling of horror (I feel it!) that one, not the most guilty, should suffer the extreme penalty while some of the most guilty and of far worse character escape with comparatively no punishment, will have a bad effect." Whether, privately, Cowburn would have liked Holdaway to be spared even from transportation we do not know, but probably not—he certainly did not ask for that degree of leniency to be shown, and in his more limited plea, despite the opposition of the Duke of Wellington, he was successful.

The Executions

Henry Cook aged 19 of Micheldever and James Thomas Cooper aged 33 of East Grimstead in Wiltshire were the two unfortunate prisoners not to be reprieved. Cook stood charged with a "felonious assault" in which two sovereigns had been taken, but more tellingly he had also knocked off the hat of William Bingham Baring JP with a sledge hammer. Cooper was charged with "riotous assembly" and machine breaking, but had also gained a certain notoriety as the self-styled 'Captain Hunt,' leading mobs around the Fordingbridge area.

At eight o'clock on the morning of Saturday 15th January, they were hanged, and all capitally convicted prisoners still in the gaol and those awaiting trial at the next Assizes were "brought out into the yard to witness the awful spectacle." Reports speak of many of the convicts weeping bitterly, some burying their faces in their smock frocks and others leaning for support against the wall of the yard unable to watch.

Submissions by Holdaway's Counsel

Although Robert Holdaway had been spared the gallows, his counsel, Charles Saunders, was still active in trying to secure his full release. He wrote to Lord Melbourne on 31st January and again in more detail the next day, enclosing affidavits and testimonials to character, and outlining the events of the 22nd and 23rd November from Holdaway's point of view.

In this he makes out the case for Holdaway's defence, including information which was not made available at the time of the trial, and puts a different perspective on the evidence submitted there. In particular he claims to have enclosed an affidavit from James Shoesmith which "favourably interprets" Holdaway's intentions during their conversation at the door of Headley Poor House; a conversation which, reported out of context, was the most serious evidence produced against Holdaway. He also notes that the fact of Holdaway's absence in the *Holly Bush* when the destruction started had not been heard at all.

But his submissions were in vain—perhaps inevitably, as Lord Melbourne in his new position had determined to take an uncharacteristically hard line to discourage further outbreaks of civil unrest—a stand in which he had the support of both King and Parliament, and which was largely successful in its desired effect.

To the Hulks

Thomas Heighes was taken from Winchester to the hulk *York* at Gosport on Tuesday 11th January, and so was not forced to witness the executions. The other eight local men sentenced to transportation were taken to the hulk later, over a period of eight days from Thursday 3rd to Thursday 10th February. The earliest of them may just have caught sight of Thomas Heighes before he sailed on Sunday 6th February for Tasmania on board the *Eliza*. Five of them (Holdaway, Triggs, Heath, James and Aaron Harding) sailed soon after on 19th February to New South Wales on board the *Eleanor*, and two (Kingshott and Thomas Harding) had to wait until 14th April to sail for Tasmania on board the *Proteus*.

The hulk 'York' in Portsmouth Harbour

For some reason James Painter was never transported; he was transferred to another hulk, the *Hardy*, on 1st March where he stayed for over two years until given a free pardon in May 1833, when he returned home to his wife and daughter in Kingsley and continued to raise a family.

While life in the hulks has often been described as being particularly grim, it is interesting to learn from an interview with another Hampshire labourer who spent two years there that he "wished he had stayed for his full 7 years." Not only were they teaching him to read, but he also found the food there far better than he could afford to buy when he returned to his native village near Sutton Scotney. "I wishes every poor, hard-working man in this here parish were as well fed with meat, and myself with them, as I wor in the hulk," he said after his release.

Hard Labour at the County Bridewell

For those imprisoned with hard labour in the County Bridewell at Winchester, life was not easy. Both Thomas and William Hoare, serving two year sentences, petitioned for early release in September 1831 on the grounds of continual ill health during their time in the gaol, but we have no record as to whether or not they were successful.

John Newland served his six months there, and we hear that early on, during bitter winter weather, his wife Ann walked from Selborne to Winchester to see him, carrying their youngest child William who was about six months old at the time. She started early but did not arrive until the following morning, and the intense cold during the night froze the baby's nose. For the rest of his life we are told William Newland's nose turned a dark blue colour and caused him great suffering in cold weather—a permanent reminder of the hard times experienced by his family and others in the year of his birth.

Transportation and After

In a New Land

All three ships transporting the local men arrived at their destinations without any incident of note, the voyages to Tasmania taking 16 weeks and that to New South Wales 18 weeks. On arrival transportees were assigned to work for various landowners, and there are records showing where each of them was sent. None of our local men ever returned.

Most seem to have avoided further trouble with the law, except for the Harding brothers. Thomas in Tasmania was found guilty in August 1838 of receiving five £1 notes knowing them to have been stolen, and in April 1839 of absconding and stealing a pair of boots. He received 12 months hard labour in chains and had his existing term of transportation extended by 2 years. Aaron in New South Wales was kept in the hulk *Phoenix* there for 11 months in 1836, an unusual length of time implying there may have been more to his detention than the stated fact that he was needed as a Crown witness.

However we also learn that Aaron started a new life for himself once he became a free man, remarrying and having two further children, Aaron born in 1845, and William born in 1848. A photograph exists of Aaron senior and his second wife holding William as a baby *(see page 66)*, and many descendants of this union now live in Australia. We have no record of any of the other local men marrying or remarrying out there.

Events Back in Hampshire

While the effect on the families of those transported must have been traumatic we can only guess at the more general outcomes the events of that week in November had on the parishes concerned, although we suspect that any financial agreements made during the disturbances were short lived.

In Selborne, the Rev E.Y. White wrote to Cowburn that he "now thought that both Mr Cobbold's prospects and life were in danger, and his friends should persuade him never to go near the place again." But vicar Cobbold stayed on for another eleven years, no better loved by his flock, and guarded by his large mastiff, until run over and killed by the Oxford Mail cart while visiting London.

The Poor House in Gracious Street was repaired, and is now known as *Fishers Buildings*. It was used again to house the local poor until 1836, when it was sold under an Act relating to the new Poor Law.

John Newland, described as a pauper in the 1841 census, seems to have become a village legend in his own lifetime. When he died in 1868 at the age of 77, the new vicar allowed him to be buried near the famous old yew tree in the churchyard at the special request of his daughter Eliza and son William, and the Trumpeter's stone stands there now to commemorate the event.

In Headley, rector Dickinson continued to be 'a good deal absent,' and we suspect well tolerated by his parishioners, for another 17 years before finding eternal peace in November 1847. The Poor House in Liphook Road was repaired, and the 1841, '51 and '61 censuses all show it still being used as such; it was sold in 1870 to a builder, who converted it into a private house, now known as *Headley Grange*. Soon after 1830 the village also started an allotment system, giving patches of land to labourers for them to grow themselves food, but wages do not seem to have risen by any significant degree.

Mary Triggs, Matthew's wife, lived on in the village to the age of 72, and died at the *Crown Inn* in 1876, surviving her husband, if she did but know it, by twenty three years. The name Triggs is still a familiar one in Headley.

ᘓ ᘓ ᘓ

Note: The text up to this point follows that of the original 1993 publication of 'One Monday in November'.

Since that time, we have discovered more details (and some corrections) concerning what happened after the riots.

This information has been added in the 'Personalities' section which follows (see page 65).

Fishers Buildings, Gracious Street, Selborne in 1992

Headley Grange, Liphook Road, Headley in 1992

In Conclusion

It cannot be said that the riots of 1830 brought any benefit to the labourers of southern England. J.L. & B. Hammond in their book *The Village Labourer 1760–1832*, written in 1911, give it as their opinion that "if the rising of 1830 had succeeded, and won back for the labourer his lost livelihood, the day when the Headley workhouse was thrown down would be remembered by the poor as the day of the taking of the Bastille." But, they continue, "this rebellion failed."

Nevertheless the events of those few days and their ramifications must have sunk deeply and painfully into the collective memories of the local villages concerned, and particularly in Selborne and Headley. Mr Laverty, who was rector of Headley from 1872 to 1929 and a tireless researcher and recorder of the village's history, seemed almost purposely to avoid the subject, and even now you sense a certain reluctance within these villages to unearth the facts supporting the legends. Legends which have grown with telling over the years.

Many facts were never recorded, some we know have been lost, and others which we have not encountered will exist. These could of course alter the interpretation we have presented here—the file is never closed on historical research—and if any readers have knowledge of their own to add to the story, the author would be most interested to hear from them.

If you live in this area, we hope the book may have told you something about the history of your locality which you were previously unaware of— and if you are from further afield, we hope it will encourage you to come and visit this beautiful and normally peaceful part of Hampshire, to see for yourself where it all happened so many years ago.

Labour Rates in 1830

Wage Scale

Labour rates in a parish were specified by local magistrates. If an employer could not, or would not, pay this rate then the labourer was given a supplement from parochial relief (the 'poor book') to bring his wages up to the required level. Parochial relief was funded by a Poor Rate, levied on all landowners in the parish at a rate determined by the Vestry (forerunner of the Parish Council) to meet local needs.

Local wages in 1830 were fixed at a maximum level of around 9/- per six-day week for an able-bodied labourer over 20 years of age, and less for labourers of lesser ability or age, according to a fixed scale. That shown below was probably typical in 1830:

			s d
Boys	from 9 to 12 Years of Age		1 - 6
	from 12 to 14 " " " " "		3 - 0
	from 14 to 16 " " " " "		4 - 0
	from 16 to 18 " " " " "		5 - 0
	from 18 to 20 " " " " "		6 - 0
Able Bodied Labourers over 20 Years of Age			9 - 0

The cry taken up throughout southern England in 1830 was for "two shillings a day" (ie. 12/- per week), but the fact that the scale above was issued for Headley parish in December 1843 shows how little the riots changed things!

If a labourer had no dependents, then all he received was the scale rate. If he was unemployed, or unemployable, then he received about 3/6d or 4/- per week "according to character" (in Alton, December 1830), although attempts were generally made by the parish to find him employment of some sort, often in mending the local roads. This would be payed at a rate somewhat lower than the scale, typically 5/- to 6/- per week.

Dependants Scale

A man on the scale rate would be expected to keep himself, a wife, and up to 2 young children on this money. If he had more children to support, then he would receive additional parochial relief according to a separate scale which varied from parish to parish, but broadly related to the price of a gallon loaf of bread per week per additional head. Such a loaf cost 1/6½ d at the time. Thus a scale proposed at Alton in December 1830 (based on a wage of 10/- per week for an able-bodied labourer) would have paid per week:

Man, wife &	3 children	0 - 11 - 6½
	4	0 - 13 - 1
	5	0 - 14 - 7½
	6	0 - 16 - 2
	7	0 - 17 - 8½

The proposal also noted that "only half the parochial relief" was to be taken off during harvest, when presumably the whole family would be expected to work.

Unemployed Men

The dependants of an unemployed man were supported entirely out of parish relief, broadly at the price of a gallon loaf of bread per person per week. In October 1827 records show that Aaron Harding, unemployed (we assume) when his wife was still alive and with six children to support, receiving 12/- a week based on the following:

> 7/- for his six children (ie. 1/2d each),
> 2/6d for his wife (Sarah),
> 2/6d for himself.

The Gallon Loaf

Wages and dependants scales were linked to the need for labourers and their families to have sufficient bread to survive, and were related to the price of a 'gallon loaf' for which we have the following recipe: 14lbs wholemeal flour, 1 gallon liquid, salt, lard, 5oz live yeast. Such a loaf would be considerably larger and more substantial than those we are used to seeing today, although in practice, we believe, smaller 'quartern' loaves were usually baked.

Nevertheless one loaf, even of the 'gallon' size, per person per week with perhaps a little bacon fat and some vegetables to go with it, can be regarded as only a bare subsistence at best.

And Beyond ...

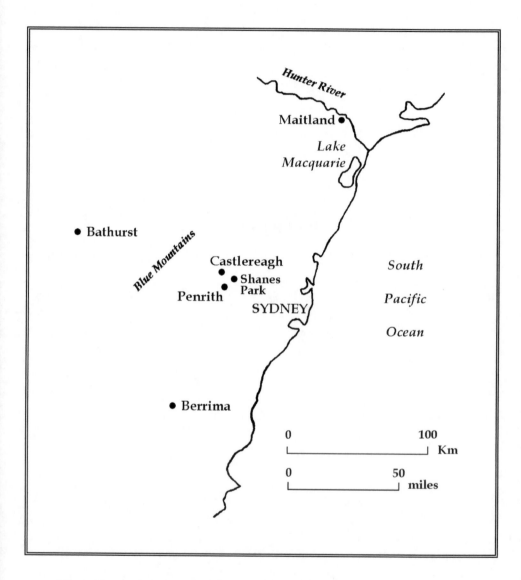

Map of locations around Sydney where some of the rioters were assigned

Australia, 1831

ஒலஒலஒல

The first colonists arrived in New South Wales in January 1788 on the 'First Fleet' – only 18 years after Captain Cook had discovered the land, and without any proper survey as to the suitability of the location for colonisation.

The situation in Britain's prisons at the time was desperate – they were overflowing – and because prisoners could no longer be shipped off to the newly-independent America, the Government decided instead to found a penal colony at Botany Bay.

Some 750 convicts, men and women, sailed from England with a detachment of marines to guard them, and remarkably all but 48 survived the eight-month journey.

Many words have been written about that voyage, and the years of near-starvation which these first colonists endured before further supplies arrived. But by the time the 'Swing' rioters appeared in 1831, nearly two generations had elapsed, free settlers had arrived and begun to live off the land, Sydney and Hobart had become recognisable as towns, and tens of thousands of convicts (or 'Government men') had been received and assimilated into the colony.

The colony on the mainland had spread some hundred miles inland and along the coasts from the original landing at Sydney, and a similar area was occupied on the island of Tasmania, or Van Diemen's Land as it was then called. By chance, the 'Swing' rioters arrived at a time when significant inroads were about to be made further into virgin territory, and their particular skills were in demand.

Status of Convicts

Convicts arriving in Australia were 'assigned' to masters for whom they worked out their sentence. They were not slaves under the law, but British citizens forced to serve a fixed term of punishment before they could become free. Often, when they had served their term, they were given land of their own, and were then themselves assigned other convicts to work on it.

Masters were required to look after their assigned convicts properly, issuing them with bedding, clothes, shelter and food. By using this system of 'assignment', the authorities not only shifted the cost and responsibility of keeping the convicts onto free settlers, but also controlled the dispersal of them within the colony, in their eyes avoiding potential rebellions. Because of this, it is unlikely that our men from Headley and Selborne met again once they had each moved to their assigned location.

The 'assignment' system also allowed the authorities to effect a 'rationing' on settlers applying for convict labour, ensuring in theory that it went where it was most needed – although this was open to much abuse, particularly when vital skills were in short supply. Blacksmiths, bricklayers and carpenters were among trades often mentioned as being scarce. Masters were not allowed to transfer convicts without permission from the authorities in Sydney or Hobart, and any who did so ran the risk of being blacklisted from getting assigned men again.

Tickets-of-Leave and Pardons

There were three ways in which convicts might be granted release from their sentence:—

A Ticket-of-Leave gave convicts the right to work and live within a given district of the colony before their sentence expired and to work on their own account, subject to good behaviour. The ticket holder was required to attend church services and to appear before a Magistrate when required. Permission was needed before moving to another district, and 'passports' were issued for this. Convicts applied for a ticket through their master, and needed to have served a stipulated portion of their sentence before one was granted. It did not give any remission on the term of the original sentence, and could be revoked at any time before the full term of the sentence had expired.

A Conditional Pardon, granted on the expiry of the term of sentence, freed convicts on the condition that they did not return to Britain.

An Absolute Pardon, issued by the Governor in certain cases, totally cleared the sentence, and allowed convicts to return home to Britain.

A Certificate of Freedom was issued at the completion of their sentence, or when a pardon of any sort was granted.

Personalities

ഒ ഒ ഒ

Known details of the 22 local men arrested, the two village clergymen, and
the London solicitor who took up Holdaway's cause, are included on the
following pages:—

Aaron & Ellis Harding holding William

Aaron Harding (c.1789–1851)
— brother of Thomas (see below) —

From convict indent:—
Age 41: ploughs, reaps, sows; of Selborne parish. Height 5ft 5¾ ins – dark ruddy complexion, black to grey hair, grey eyes, third finger of right hand crooked at point. Could read. Married. Warrant dated 4th December 1830: Riotous assembly and destruction of Selborne Union. Sentence: Death, commuted to life transportation. Received on hulk *York* 5th February 1831, sailed on *Eleanor*.

There is evidence to support the view that Aaron Harding was one of the prime perpetrators of the riot in Selborne—probably more so than Robert Holdaway. At his trial, people accused him of having a prominent role, and he was certainly in trouble before the riot occurred, having been in the courts three times and in jail twice:—

- Easter 1822 – aged 32. Committed on 30th March 1822 by James Battin Coulthard Esq for six weeks imprisonment to hard labour, for having run away and left his wife and family chargeable to the parish of Selborne.
- Epiphany 1822 – aged 32. Committed on 23rd December 1822 by Henry Budd Esq for three calendar months imprisonment to hard labour, for a misdemeanour.
- Easter 1827 – aged 37. Committed on 16th January 1827, by the Rev E White for refusing to find sureties for his appearance at the next General Quarter Sessions of the Peace, for an assault. Acquitted.

Vicar Cobbold, at least, was convinced that Aaron should not be reprieved from his sentence after the riot and, hearing rumours that a petition had been got up on behalf of him and John Heath, wrote to Lord Melbourne on 28th January 1831 stating that they were *"the most desperate and daring characters of his entire parish and the terror of the neighbourhood, and should they be let loose on society again there is no saying what may happen."* (See section on John Heath for full text of the letter)

Aaron was indeed a colourful character, as his subsequent life in Australia proved.

Born near East Worldham around 1789 (we have not found a record of his baptism), son of William and Mary Harding, he married Sarah Stacey at East Worldham on 7th August 1810.

They had nine children (ages in 1830): William (20), Mary Ann (18), George (16), Henry (14), Daniel (11), James (9), Elizabeth (6), Maria (4) and Thomas (2)—all baptised at Selborne.

His wife had died in June 1829 aged 44, and was buried at Selborne.

After transportation, Aaron was assigned to John Atkinson near Berrima in a district then called Sutton Forest, about 80 miles south-west of Sydney. We know a little about Atkinson: he called his property Mereworth, and established an Inn called the *Kentish Arms* there. But he eventually ran into financial trouble, and sold Mereworth and left the district in the 1840s. The *Kentish Arms*, later renamed the *Three Legs o' Man*, was demolished in the early 1900s.

Aaron was kept in the hulk *Phoenix*[†] in Sydney Harbour for 11 months from 29 January 1836 as witness for the Crown, though we have yet to discover the reason why. We also note that in March 1835 there was a letter addressed to an 'Aron' Harding lying unclaimed at the GPO in Sydney, according to the NSW Government Gazette of the time (see also John Heath).

He 'married' Alice (Ellis) Sargent at Sutton Forest between 3rd July 1843 and the end of 1844. She already had 9 children of her own. In fact the marriage probably never happened, as there is no evidence of Alice's divorce from her husband Thomas Sargent or of her marriage to Aaron, but she and Aaron had a child, also Aaron, born 26th September 1845 at Sutton Forest.

Alice had the custody of the four younger children from her first marriage, Henry (5), Jane (4), Mary (3) and James (21 months), and with the five children, she and Aaron decided to pioneer across to South Australia. It is not known what route was taken, some say they followed the river (possibly Murrumbidgee) until they met up with the Murray/Darling, then followed the Murray through to Adelaide. Others say they blazed their own trail with a herd of cattle, which took from 6 months to two years. The latter is most likely as Aaron Harding called himself an overlander at the time. A rifle said to be one used on the trip over from NSW is now in the possession of a great grandson of Henry Sargent.

However, we know that the family was settled in Gawler by June 1848, as the baptism of Aaron and Alice's second child was recorded there. William Harding was born on the 2nd April 1848, but no birth certificate can be found. He was baptised at St George's Church, Gawler on 4th June 1848, by Rev WH Coombs, their address being Floraville, S.A. Due to their broad English accents, the baptism of William was registered as William 'Arden'.

While they were living at Gawler, Aaron Harding senior was found dead on his property on 6th November 1851. An inquest resulted, with the finding of "accidental death." Henry Sargent, who would have been only 11 years old at the time, was called as a witness, calling himself Henry Harden.

[†] *The 600 ton 'Phoenix' was the only hulk ever to operate in Australia. She ran aground entering Port Jackson in 1824, was damaged beyond repair, and commissioned as a prison hulk in 1826. Witnesses waiting to testify before the Sydney courts were routinely confined there and taken across daily to attend the hearings. ['The Larrikins of Lavender Bay', Beverley Earnshaw]*

Aaron's name was registered as Harden for the inquest. A search for the death certificate of Aaron Harding (Harden) has so far failed.

On 12th June 1852, Alice (Ellis) re-married to Richard Rees, bullock driver of Peachy Belt, Gawler Plains. At this time she was calling herself Alice Arden, widow. She died on 21st October 1863 at Butchers Gap, her death being registered by her son Henry.

There is an unsubstantiated family story that Richard Rees destroyed his wife's will when she died, and kicked Aaron junior and William Harding out with only the clothes they stood up in. Whatever the truth, they survived, and went on to ensure that Aaron Harding of Hampshire contributed 18 grandchildren and 35 great grand-children to the population of his new homeland. The majority of Aaron's Australian descendants now live in or around the suburbs of Adelaide, and the rest are scattered across the country.

Aaron Harding Sources: Marjorie Burwood, Jill Chambers, Lynn Croucher, Hilda Symonds, Geof Watts and others

Descendants of Aaron HARDING (in England)

1 Aaron HARDING 1789–1851
+Sarah STACEY 1786–1829
  2 William HARDING 1810–
  2 Mary Ann HARDING 1812–
  2 George HARDING 1814–
   +Anne EADE
   3 George HARDING 1840–
   3 Sarah HARDING 1842–
   3 Mary Ann HARDING 1846-
   3 William HARDING 1849–
  2 Henry HARDING 1816–1862
   +Mary Ann PINK 1820–
   3 Mary Ann HARDING 1840–1856
   3 Ellen HARDING 1841–1858
   3 Henry HARDING 1843–
   3 Jane HARDING 1844–1936
    +Allen PUNTER 1841–1926
    4 Alan PUNTER 1866–
    4 Albert PUNTER 1868–
    4 Thomas PUNTER 1874–
    4 Percy PUNTER 1878–
    4 Ethel PUNTER 1884–1967
     +John FRANKLIN 1883–1972
     5 John FRANKLIN 1909–1987
     5 Ethel FRANKLIN 1911–
     5 Marjorie FRANKLIN 1923–
      +Francis BURWOOD 1921–
       (1 offspring)

   3 Elizabeth HARDING 1846–
   3 William HARDING 1849–
   3 Thomas HARDING 1852–1875
   3 Eliza Maria HARDING 1855–
   3 Edward HARDING 1857–
   3 Frederick HARDING 1860–
   3 Alice HARDING 1863–
  2 Daniel HARDING 1819–
  2 James HARDING 1821–
   +Jane PAYNE
   3 Eliza HARDING 1846
   3 Louisa HARDING 1847
   3 William Henry HARDING 1848
   3 Phoebe HARDING 1850
   3 James George HARDING 1853
  2 Elizabeth HARDING 1824–
   +John COLLYER?
  2 Maria HARDING 1826–
   +William EADE
   3 Fanny EADE
  2 Thomas HARDING 1828–1855
   +Elizabeth DILLING

Australian line continued over /...

Descendants of Aaron HARDING (in Australia)

1 **Aaron HARDING 1789–1851**
+2nd Wife of Aaron HARDING: Ellis (Alice) PACKHAM 1806–1863

2 Aaron HARDING 1845–1928
 +Margaret BROWN 1850–1928
  3 William James HARDING 1872–1950
   +Lois Rebecca WEBB 1876–1970
    4 Mildred Venetta HARDING 1898–1960
     +Ernest Hugo HAMMERLING 1881–1940
      (1 offspring)
    4 Lindsay Clarence HARDING 1901–
     +Rose Isobelle STACEY 1903–
      (3 offspring)
    4 Eric James HARDING 1905–
    4 Walter George HARDING 1914–
     +Thora GERSCH 1917–
      (7 offspring)
    4 William Ronald HARDING 1917–
     +Kathleen CAGNEY 1910–
      (1 offspring)
  3 George Aaron HARDING 1874–1970
   +Elsie Mabel BENSCH 1881–1976
    4 Constance HARDING 1909–1911
    4 Trixie May HARDING 1911–1950
     +Arthur Edward Douglas FREEMAN
                           1910–1991
      (2 offspring)
    4 Melva Mavis HARDING 1914–2000
     +Donald McLachlan CAMPBELL
                           1911–1965
      (4 offspring)
    4 Gwenda Audrey HARDING 1916–1968
     +Donald George BROWN 1914–1942
      (1 offspring)
     +Frederick Norman WATTS 1915–1973
      (3 offspring)
    4 Una Margaret HARDING 1918–
     +Raymond ROBINSON 1920–
  3 Elizabeth Alice HARDING 1876–1956
   +Arthur John WEBB 1872–1956
    4 Laurence Arthur WEBB 1909–
     +Emma-Anna Wanda HAMDORF 1907–
      (4 offspring)
    4 Doris Edith WEBB 1907–
     +Charlie Cecil WISHART 1904–
      (3 offspring)

  3 Emma Jane HARDING 1878–1959
  3 Margaret Ethel HARDING 1880–
   +William Michael BESANKO 1873–1928
    4 Walter Wilbur BESANKO 1909–
    4 Leslie Harding BESANKO 1912–
     +Inez Edna THOMAS 1912–
      (1 offspring)
     +Selina Elizabeth GREEN 1917–
    4 Edith Margaret BESANKO 1916–
    4 Laurel Evelyn BESANKO 1922–
     +Douglas Walter GOLDING 1916–
      (3 offspring)
  3 Walter Ridley HARDING 1882–1905
  3 Elsie Mabel HARDING 1886–1968
  3 Eva Mary HARDING 1887–1940
   +Ernest BEANEY 1871–1942
  3 Ada Evelyn HARDING 1890–
   +Alexander William DAVEY –1960
    4 Nancy Evelyn DAVEY 1918–
     +Harold Leigh BEANEY 1909–
      (2 offspring)
    4 Shirley Margaret DAVEY 1925–
     +Allan FOOT 1920–1969
  3 Lindsay Harold HARDING 1892–1897

2 William HARDING 1848–1930
 +Honor Edwards POLKINHORN 1851–1909
  3 Hilda May HARDING 1892–1893
 *2nd Wife of William HARDING:
 +Emily PITMAN 1875–1952
  3 Hilda May HARDING 1915–
   +Alec James SYMONDS 1916–1971
    4 Peter John SYMONDS 1942–
     + Rosemay Kane BEST 1943–
     + Jill Rosalyn HURLEY 1944–
    4 Judith Margaret Adair SYMONDS 1945–
     +Robin Howe BLAIR 1942–
      (2 offspring)

70

Thomas Harding (1798– at least 1842)

— brother of Aaron (see above) —

From convict indent:—
Age 32: can plough, reap, thresh and milk; of Kingsley parish. Height 5ft 5 ins – dark complexion, dark brown hair, grey eyes. Single. Warrant dated 4th December 1830: Riotous assembly and beginning the destruction of Headley Union. No former convictions. Sentence: Death, commuted to seven years transportation. Received on the hulk *York* 10th February 1831, sailed on *Proteus*.
(Note that there were two Thomas Hardings on the *Proteus*.)

Thomas Harding was baptised in Kingsley on 24th June 1798, son of William and Mary, and younger brother of Aaron. He was still single at the time of the riot.

In Tasmania, he was assigned to the service of Dr Henderson in the north of the island, almost certainly in Launceston. His ticket of leave was granted on 8th September 1835, and his free pardon (presumably a Conditional Pardon) dated 3rd February 1836. He would then have been eligible for a Certificate of Freedom on 27th December 1837, seven years after his initial conviction.

Instead, he seems to have started to run foul of the law. George Rudé, in a lecture he gave during 1970, called him an 'adventurous spirit' and reports his exploits thus:—

He seems to have been a good worker and had no record of offences in the colony at the time of his free pardon in February 1836. But, two years later, he was found guilty of receiving five stolen £1 notes and sentenced at the Launceston quarter sessions to seven years' transportation. In November 1838, he absconded from a road party and a £2 reward was offered for his capture. Brought to trial again, his sentence was extended by another two years. Once more, he absconded—this time from the custody of a constable who was escorting him from Hobart Town to Bridgewater in May 1839. He seems, this time, to have been more successful, as his name features on the half-yearly lists of absconders for July 1840, and again in January and July 1842. And that as far as I can discover, is the last we hear of him!

Indeed, it is the last that anyone has been able to learn of him. Family rumours exist saying that he managed to escape from Tasmania, even that he may have returned to England—but no-one knows for sure.

Thomas Harding Sources: *Jill Chambers, George Rudé, Geoff Sharman, Geof Watts*

John Heath (1788–at least 1837)

From convict indent:—
Age stated as 45 (actually 42): farm carpenter; Cobbold said he was 'a master carpenter of Selborne parish with a house and a shop'. Height 5ft 6½ ins – dark ruddy complexion, dark brown hair, hazel-grey eyes, missing point of third finger on left hand. Education 'none'. Single. Warrant dated 30th November 1830: Riotous assembly and destruction of Headley Union. No former convictions. Sentence: Death, commuted to life transportation. Received on the hulk *York* 8th February 1831, sailed on *Eleanor*.

John was born in Selborne on 29th November 1788, baptised 4th January 1789, the eldest of thirteen children of John and Charlotte Heath. He had not married at the time of the riot.

Of his siblings, it is interesting to note that Robert, born 13th May 1794, married Ellen Newland, daughter of the 'Trumpeter' John Newland, on 30th May 1847. Ellen was tried in March 1849 for the attempted murder of Robert, and transported to Tasmania with their baby daughter. *(See below under John Newland).*

This Robert wrote to William Cowburn following John's sentence asking for help in acquitting him:—

Selbourn Jany 12th

> *Dear Sir i have taken the Liberty of Wrighting to You about my Brother John Heath who is to be Transported for Life   Sir if You Can Speak to do any Good for My Brother it Will be my endeavour to Satesfiy You as far as Lays in My Power Robert Heath.*
>
> *Charles Bennett as Sworn again him for being up on Headley poorhouse but thear are 9 or 10 People that will Come on their Oath that John was never in the House at all.*
>
> *Sir we have been to the Rev^nd Mr Wells and he says if you think a pettion whould Do Good for my Brother he whould Draw one up for us so Dear Sir if you can make it conveint to send me a few Lines I will endeavur to satesfy You for it.*
>
> *Robert Heath*

There had also been a number of sworn affidavits on John Heath's behalf, from Sarah Adams, Joseph Cobb, Charlotte Heath (his mother), Andrew Knight, Thomas Ralfs and Hori Smith.

Charlotte Heath said: *On Monday morning the twenty second day of November last her son John Heath was taken from his shop by about fifty or sixty men who came there and insisted on the said John Heaths going with them or they would pull down his shop wherein he was then at work.*

Sarah Adams, a 'widow of Selborne', said that she was *standing by the gate of the Headley Poorhouse premises for about one hour whilst the men were engaged in doing injury to the Poorhouse—that she saw John Heath come from off the Common and stood resting on his stick by the Gate near to her and she verily believes that he did not go into the Poorhouse during any part of the time that the injury was done, she having stood near to him all the time and must have seen him advance towards the said Poorhouse if he had done so.* (Interesting to note that this implies some women from Selborne, as well as their men, may have been present at the Headley riot).

Thomas Ralfs, labourer of the parish of Kingsley, gave another view of the Headley sacking, saying that he *was standing just within the outer gate of the Headley Poorhouse premises whilst the mob were engaged in breaking off the tiles of the said House—that whilst he was advancing a few paces towards the House by the footpath John Heath came hastily after him and caught hold of him and said "you come back and stop along with me"—* whereupon he and John Heath *retired about three yards and stood still near the outer gate in the footpath.* Whilst they were standing there Heath said to him, *"there is Charles Bennett pushing the tiles off, see his head through the roof, he sweats like a Bull."* Ralfs confirms this, saying that *Charles Bennett was on the roof of the poorhouse taking a very active part in the destruction thereof and altho Charles Bennett swore upon the Trial that John Heath was upon the roof of the Poorhouse,* Ralfs 'verily believes' that *the said John Heath was not on the roof of the Poorhouse nor did he in his opinion take any part in the destruction thereof,* he having seen him *retire from the said footpath into the Road at the time the said mob left the said Poorhouse for Kingsley.*

However, the vicar of Selborne was adamant that John Heath should not be reprieved, and wrote to Lord Melbourne against remission *(see also Aaron Harding)*:—

Jany 28, 1831

My Lord,

A report has reached me today, that a recommendation has been made to your Lordship in favour of John Heath, who with Aaron Harding, was convicted at the late Special Commission at Winchester, of being concerned in demolishing the Headley Workhouse, and had both of them sentence of death recorded against them. I know not whether the report is true or not, but it is from an apprehension and alarm that it may be true, that I take the liberty of imploring your Lordship, to listen with great caution to any recommendation, come from what quarter it may, which has for its object any remission of the sentence of either of these men, which the Judges assured me should be transported for life, as they are the most desperate and daring character of my whole parish, and the terror of the neighbourhood, and should they be let loose on society again, there is no saying, what may happen.

I am, my Lord,
yr lordship's obed ser Wm Cobbold
Vicar of Selborne

There is a note on the letter, *'Inform that Ld M has no intention of recomd for mercy.'*

On arrival in New South Wales in July 1831, John Heath was assigned to Capt James St John Ranclaud who held a large estate called 'Trialba' at Teralba on Lake Macquarie, about 100 miles up the coast north of Sydney. This estate 'extended west from the mouth of Cockle Creek to the foothills of the Sugarloaf Range, at Killingworth.'

Capt Ranclaud died on 29th May 1832, and the grant passed to his son, James Ranclaud junior—but it seems that prior to this, according to a letter from the Resident Magistrate at Maitland dated 2nd May 1832, John Heath had been *removed from the service of Captain Ranclaud in consequence of his having improperly transferred this man to Mr Simpson for a period of twelve months*—which would indicate that Heath had hardly worked for Ranclaud at all.

Mr Simpson was probably Percy Simpson, an Assistant Surveyor of Roads and Bridges for a number of years from 1828, who owned land on the south western side of Lake Macquarie and was instrumental in the construction of the Great North Road.

In July 1832, we find a 'Henry Heath' of the *Eleanor*, described as a 'rough carpenter', attached to the Government's No.29 Road party building the Long Bridge at Maitland, up the Hunter River from the Ranclaud estate. Since there was only one Heath on the *Eleanor*, and John was indeed a carpenter, we assume he was the man.

By the following month, August 1832, he had been assigned yet again (the New South Wales Government Gazette describing him this time as 'Eleanor Heath', farm carpenter) to another master, Lieut Hanbury Clements of Drummond Ville near Liverpool, about 15 miles west of Sydney.

Clements had served in the Navy from 1812, then chartered a boat to emigrate to Australia with his family in 1828—where they arrived eventually, having survived ship-wreck at the Cape of Good Hope. By 1830, he had been granted land at Summerhill Estate near Bathurst, 120 miles inland, and a six-day journey from Sydney over the Blue Mountains—an area which had only just been opened up for settlers within the previous decade. It was here that John Heath was employed.

He is recorded as being there in the 1837 Muster, and from there he petitioned on 27th February 1837 to see if he was pardoned—the reply being, *John Heath is not named in the list received from the Col. Sec. of State.*

His Conditional Pardon was, in fact, dated 9th November 1837, but we know that he had not collected it by June 1850, and we have as yet no further details of his life.

In a list of unclaimed letters at Sydney GPO issued in March 1835, there is one addressed to a John Heath. We wonder if it was 'our' John Heath, and whether it was ever collected.

Heath Sources: *Jill Chambers, Geof Watts*

Thomas Heighes (1801–1838)

— brother of William (see below) —

From convict indent:—
Age 29: farm labourer, of Shortheath, Selborne parish. Height 5ft 8¾ ins – brown complexion, brown hair, grey eyes. Warrant dated 29th November 1830: Charged with having, on the 24th day of November instant, at Week (Wyck) in the parish of Binsted, maliciously damaged, with intent to destroy, a threshing machine, the property of Robert Shotter and Edward Baigent, of the value of twenty-five pounds. Sentence: seven years transportation. Received on the hulk *York* 11th January 1831, sailed on *Eliza*.

Thomas Heighes was born in Selborne parish on 1st August 1801, and baptised on 25th October 1801, the sixth child (second son) of William and Sarah. He married Ann Bright at Selborne on 20th June 1822, and they had two children (ages in 1830): Lucy (3) and James (1).

In Tasmania, he worked for Mr Solomon Austin (1833) and Thomas Hughes (1835). His ticket of leave was granted on 1st June 1835, and his free pardon dated 3rd February 1836.

It is recorded that a 'Thomas Heyes' died on 27th December 1838, of fever, in the John Kelsh Colonial Hospital, Hobart. The informant was the hospital Superintendent. His age is recorded as being 38 years and he was a labourer. The death was registered the next day.

William Heighes (1799–1889)

— brother of Thomas (see above) —

Age 30: of Shortheath, Selborne parish. Charge same as Thomas above. Committed to gaol week ending 4th December 1830, but acquitted with a severe reprimand.
　　Family legend says that another brother, John Heighes, escaped capture only by chance—'the necessity of going into Alton to dispose of a hare leading him to avoid the rioters.'

William Heighes was born in Selborne parish in 1799, fifth child and eldest son of William and Sarah. He married Elizabeth Cole at Selborne on 11th November 1824, and they had three children at the time of the riot (ages in 1830): William (4), James (4), Sarah (born January 1830). After his acquittal, eight other children were born.

According to the 1843 tithe map, William and his family were living at Waterside, Oakhanger, a small farm on the edge of Shortheath Common, its eastern boundary being a bend in the Oakhanger stream. The boundary is still exactly the same today, though the old house is no longer there. In 1843, the farm belonged to William's mother and in her will of 1847 (she died in 1850) there is no mention of William, but all of the other children then living shared equally. We suspect a family quarrel, but have no evidence to support this.

William emigrated to Canada in 1850 with his family—one child had died before the family left, and seven are recorded as arriving with their parents in New York on 1st July 1850. The two eldest sons, William and James are thought to have arrived in advance.

William Heighes and his sister Elizabeth, born in Canada, grandchildren of William Heighes the rioter

William the patriarch died in his 90th year, on 13th February 1889 at Holland Township, Ontario. A considerable number of his descendants live today in Canada and the USA.

Heighes Sources: *John Heighes, Geoff Sharman*

Robert Holdaway (1790–1853)

From convict indent:—

Age stated as 37 (actually 40): carpenter, wheelwright, hop-planter, ex-publican, of Selborne parish. Height 5ft 5½ ins – ruddy complexion, brown hair turning grey, hazel-grey eyes, a small scar at each end of left eyebrow and a small raised mole under left side of mouth. Could read and write. Married. Warrant dated 26th November 1830: Riotous assembly and destruction of Headley Union. No former convictions. Sentence: Death, reprieved 8th January 1831, commuted to life transportation. Received on hulk *York* 9th February 1831, sailed on *Eleanor*.

Most of what was known initially about Robert Holdaway came from 'interested parties' of one persuasion or another. There was the prosecution's evidence at his trial, given by the Master of Headley Workhouse and by William Cobbold, the unloved vicar of Selborne; and the subsequent statement by his defence counsel which tried to put a different complexion on the same facts. All were potentially biased.

Then we found the records of William Cowburn, a London solicitor living with his family in Selborne in 1830. He was in London at the time of the riot, but his wife wrote daily from Selborne telling him what was going on. He took up Holdaway's cause in order to prevent him from being hanged, as he felt this would be disruptive of village life in Selborne. However he was quite happy, it seems, to see him transported. From the correspondence of Cowburn with others during this time we get some unsolicited views on Holdaway's character.

One example is from Edmund Yalden White, great-nephew of the naturalist Gilbert White, writing from Crondall on 2nd January 1831:—

To William Cowburn, Esq. I write this to say how rejoiced I am to find you espousing poor Holdaway's cause. I view the whole subject in exactly the same light as yourself. I have had several transactions with Holdaway and always found him a well-behaved, civil, honest, obliging peaceable and respectful man, and shall always be ready and happy to <u>say</u> so or to <u>write</u> so if it will in any way assist your cause; and may God grant you success.

I told many of my friends yesterday that I thought both Mr Cobbold's prospects and life were in danger, and his friends should persuade him never to go near the place again.

Born in Ovington in 1790, the fifth son (and eighth child) of John and Mary Holdaway, Robert married Elizabeth Jane Mayhew at Bighton, near Alresford, on 8th July 1813. They had three children (ages in 1830): Mary Ann (17), William Mayhew (14) and John Freeborn (12) — all born in Bighton.

Elizabeth died in February 1820 aged 25 years, and Robert married Sarah Freeman, a minor then 18 years old, daughter of a respected Alresford butcher, at New Alresford on 5th July 1821. They had five children (ages in 1830) Jane (8), Sarah (7), Frederick Robert (4), Frances (3) and Elizabeth Mary (1) — all but Jane were born in Selborne.

Robert was transported on the *Eleanor*, which set sail from Portsmouth on 19th February 1831 with a total of 203 on board and arrived at Port Jackson on 29th June, the surgeon remarking in his Journal that *"no set of men perhaps under similar circumstances ever suffered less from disease, the names of eleven convicts only appear on the general list of sick and of these several might with great propriety have been omitted."* One of these was Robert Holdaway who, along with the Cook, had suffered a 'trifling' scald and was kept in the sick bay for eleven days!

On arrival in Australia, Robert worked for Dr John Harris, seemingly as a wheelwright, first at Shane's Park Estate on South Creek, then at Penrith. We have a description of the place and of Dr Harris, then aged 77, who had been a surgeon with the Second Fleet, and was the first doctor to settle and practice in Australia — *Shane's Park is one of the prettiest places in the County of Cumberland. There is a beautiful stretch of the South Creek about one mile long and eighty to one hundred yards wide, the orchard terraced from the top of the bank to the water's edge very prettily. Dr Harris was a cripple, or paralysed in his legs, and had to be lifted in and out of a small vehicle made to wheel him about. Mrs Eliza Harris was a fine lady-like looking woman, and one beloved by all her servants.*[†]

Unfortunately, we can find no records to tell us more about Robert Holdaway in Australia, but we do know that he wrote home in 1831, with Dr Harris's permission, asking for his wife and children to join him.

A letter from William Cobbold to Lord Melbourne, dated 1st March 1832, reads: *My Lord, Robert Holdaway, late of this Parish, of notorious memory on account of the leading part he took in the riots in this neighbourhood at the close of the year 1830, for which he was sentenced to death which sentence was afterwards commuted to transportation for life, has lately written home to his wife, expressing a strong wish that she and her family of eight children will go over to him, which she has signified to the Parish a great desire to comply with, provided they will defray the expense of her passage. But as they think the sum of money which would be required for this would be greater than they could afford, I write to your Lordship at their bequest, to ask whether Government would not assist them in [...]ring the object of their wishes in getting rid of such a heavy drain upon their funds — or whether they could not put them in a way of getting assistance from some other quarter.*

[†] From *Dharug & Dungaree: The History of Penrith and St Marys to 1860* written by Robert Murray and Kate White (published 1988)

79

There is another letter dated 23rd October 1833 from J. Dunn, Under Sheriff at Alresford, which reads:—

The wife of Holdaway whom you know was transported for life being one of the Selborne rioters has just been with me in great distress to implore me to use every exertion to get leave for her and her five infant children to join her husband at Sydney. I believe I once applied to you on this subject and your reply was that the government would not consent to it except some assurance could be given that they would not become burdensome to the colony, but since I am told that the higher powers have relaxed in this resolution and that some of the parties who were transported for limited periods have actually been set at liberty and Mrs Holdaway confirms this by declaring she had seen two of them (natives of Stratton) and that they came through Alresford on their way home—she has shown me a letter she has just received from her husband urging her to join him and assuring her that he has ample means of supporting her five children and he further states that his master has sent a certificate of his good character to entitle him to this favour.

The wife is the daughter of Freeman the butcher of this place who is a respectable man, but with an extremely large family, and he is likewise very pressing in his desire to accomplish his daughter's wishes. I hope therefore you will be able to give me some hope and expectation that a licence may be given for her departure to New South Wales—we could get a petition strongly signed by the Selborne people if that would aid the cause and the overseers no doubt would contribute largely towards the expense of the voyage.

But, for whatever reason, Sarah did not go to Australia, and eventually she re-married in 1843 (see below).

Robert was granted a conditional pardon dated 9th November 1837, but he seems not to have collected it, according to the list issued by the Principal Superintendent of Convicts' Office, Sydney in June 1850. His name also appears on a memorandum issued by the Colonial Secretary's Office in Sydney, dated 8th June 1838, authorising payment of £4 to him from Savings Bank. On this document, his 'condition' is stated as 'free'.

Robert Holdaway died in 1853 and is believed to be buried in Camperdown, Sydney.

———————

From a talk given in October 1996 to a meeting of the Selborne Association, by Nigel Mulcaster, great-great-great-grandson of Robert Holdaway.

At the time of the riot, Robert lived at Selborne with his second wife Sarah and his eight children, three by a first marriage. After his transportation, Sarah moved away and the 1841 census shows her living in Windmill Row, Alverstoke, Gosport, with three daughters—and a young grandson, Charles, who had been born to her 15 year-old daughter Jane earlier that year. On

30th September 1843 Sarah married a widower, Eli Newman, and went to live with him in Farringdon, back near Selborne again. He already had four children of his own, and in 1846 they had a daughter, Emma Lavinia.

Sadly, in May 1869, Sarah Newman, as she then was, took her own life. The incident was reported in the *Hampshire Chronicle* as follows:—

SUICIDE BY A FEMALE—An inquest was held at Farringdon on Thursday se'nnight before Mr H Harfield, deputy county coroner, on the body of Sarah Newman, aged 67 years, the wife of Eli Newman, a labourer. It appeared that the deceased had complained very much of late of pains in her head, and at times became very weak and nervous, hardly knowing what she said or did. Her husband left her at six o'clock on the previous Monday morning, and when he returned to dinner found the doors fastened from the inside. He obtained assistance from a neighbour, and on the back door being broken open they found the deceased hanging by a rope to a beam in the washhouse. There was a chair by the side of her, on which she had apparently stepped to fasten the rope to the beam. Her husband cut her down, but she was then quite dead. The jury returned a verdict of 'suicide while in a state of unsound mind.'

It seems a tragic end for a woman who had such a hard life, and was unable to join Robert in Australia with her children because she could not raise the money.

Sarah is buried in Farringdon churchyard next to the old yew tree. Her gravestone is also dedicated to the memory of her husband Eli, who died on 26th September 1878, aged 80, but we have subsequently found that he is buried at Church Crookham without a headstone.

Sarah & Eli Newman's gravestone, viewed from inside the old yew tree at Farringdon Churchyard

My great-great-grandfather, Frederick Robert Holdaway, was Robert's third child by his marriage to Sarah, and was four years old when his father was transported. He appears on the 1841 census in New Alresford living with his mother's brother Richard Freeman, a butcher.

In 1843 he joined the Royal Navy and changed his surname to HOLLOWAY, possibly because he was embarrassed about his father's convict record. He did his boys training at *HMS Fisgard* and served on a number of ships including *Penguin*, *Siren*, *Madagascar*, *Impregnable*, *Dauntless* and *Irresistible*. He passed his exams for boatswain in 1856. We do not know if he was involved in any battles or if he was awarded any medals.

While in Plymouth in 1847 he married Ann Tremeer. On his marriage certificate he not only retained the surname HOLLOWAY for himself, but gave it as his father's surname too. Frederick and Ann had four children, namely Emily Elizabeth, Anne, Frederick William (my great grandfather) and Alice Jane.

Later in Frederick's naval career, the family moved to Worthing and he joined the coast guard, at this time part of the navy. He retired from the navy in 1869 on a pension of £36 17s per annum, and worked for the Surveyor's Office at Worthing Town Hall for nearly twelve years, receiving a reference in 1881 saying that he had proved himself to be a thoroughly steady, honest, hard working man and a good servant in every respect.

Some time between then and 1888, he moved with his wife and youngest daughter to Alton. His wife died on 10th March 1888 and is buried in Alton Cemetery. In the 1891 census we find him living on his own in Young's Cottage, and he had changed his surname back to HOLDAWAY. He died of 'senile decay' on 26th May 1898 aged 72 and was buried with his wife. He had purchased the grave under the name of Holloway, and his wife was buried as a Holloway. In the burial book at Alton Cemetery there is a pencilled note saying, 'rather a query over the name'!

Their daughter Alice Jane married Alfred James Simpson at Alton in 1890 also under the surname Holloway. This couple had nine children, and there are probably descendants living in the Alton area now who might be trying to trace their ancestors with the name of Holloway without much success. We have been in touch with one, who was amazed to hear the story.

Their son, Frederick William, was born in Plymouth in 1861 and also joined the Navy like his father. He served for twelve years and left the service in 1890 as an Able Seaman. He married in 1911 and changed his name back to HOLDAWAY. He had four sons and a daughter—my grandfather Frederick Robert Holdaway being born in 1912. Frederick Robert died in Guildford as recently as 1992, the year before Mr Smith published his book *One Monday in November*—if only he had known, he could have picked up the phone during his research and spoken to him.

Holdaway Sources: *Jill Chambers, Keith Holdaway, Christine Mulcaster, Nigel Mulcaster*

Frederick Robert Holdaway, born 1826, eldest son of Robert & Sarah;
joined the Royal Navy in 1843 and changed his surname to HOLLOWAY

Descendants of Robert HOLDAWAY

1 Robert HOLDAWAY 1790–1853
+Elizabeth Jane MAYHEW 1794–1820
2 Mary Ann HOLDAWAY 1813–1869
2 William Mayhew HOLDAWAY 1816–1903
+Elizabeth KNIGHT –1874
*2nd Wife of William Mayhew HOLDAWAY:
+Emma BROOMFIELD 1856–1918
3 William Mayhew HOLDAWAY 1875–1962
+Lucy HART 1860–1947
3 Arthur HOLDAWAY 1877–1877
2 John Freeborn HOLDAWAY 1818–1882
+Sarah (Sally) BUNNY 1818–1908
3 Harriet Jane HOLDAWAY 1852–1916
+Walter George GREENWOOD 1852–1932
3 Frederick John HOLDAWAY 1858–1937
+Mary Ann –1937
3 George Phillip HOLDAWAY 1861–1861
+Sarah FREEMAN 1803–1869 (2nd Wife)
2 Jane HOLDAWAY 1822–
3 Francis Charles HOLDAWAY 1841–
+James SMITH
2 Sarah HOLDAWAY 1823–1885
+John ORTON –1892
3 Emma ORTON 1846–
+Frederick EVANS
4 Sarah EVANS 1866–
4 Emma EVANS 1872–
4 Frederick EVANS 1875–
2 Frederick Robert HOLDAWAY/HOLLOWAY
1826–1898
+Ann TREMEER 1827–1888
3 Emily Elizabeth HOLLOWAY 1848–1926
+Frederick HINTON 1846–1914
4 Annie HINTON 1871–
4 Frederick HINTON 1873–
4 William HINTON 1875–
4 Alice HINTON 1879–
4 Ethel Newcome HINTON 1882–
3 Ann L HOLLOWAY
3 Frederick Robert HOLLOWAY/HOLDAWAY
1861–1940
+Anne Alice CARTER 1879–1955
4 Frederick Robert HOLDAWAY 1912–1992
+Gertrude Edith LEWER
5 Ann HOLLOWAY 1937–1938
*2nd Wife of Frederick Robert HOLDAWAY:
+Irene Margaret DURANT 1923–1947
5 Christine HOLDAWAY 1947–
+Peter Michael MULCASTER 1944–
*3rd Wife of Frederick Robert HOLDAWAY:
+Rebecca Elizabeth RICHARDSON 1915–1986
4 William Arthur HOLDAWAY 1913–1921
4 Jack Edward HOLDAWAY 1914–1993
+Gwendoline COLLYER –1996

4 Frank Butler HOLDAWAY 1918–1981
4 Gertrude Alice HOLDAWAY 1919–1972
+James Ronald Gerard DALE 1919–2000
5 Lynne DALE 1946–
+Roy ENTICKNAP
3 Alice Jane HOLLOWAY 1862–1936
+Alfred James SIMPSON 1860–1906
4 Robert William SIMPSON 1891–1934
+Helen Mary CONSTABLE –1981
5 Mary Helen SIMPSON 1929–
4 Alice Ann SIMPSON 1892–1976
4 Helena Louise SIMPSON 1895–
4 Ethel Mary SIMPSON 1896–
+Edwin James BOWERS
4 Edith Frances SIMPSON 1896–1946
4 Alfred Frederick SIMPSON 1897–1901
4 Joy Anne SIMPSON 1899–1927
4 Kathleen SIMPSON 1902–
+Leslie Samuel Everard JAGO
5 Michael Leslie JAGO 1936–1986
+Dierdre Minchington FLETT 1940–
4 Arthur James SIMPSON 1905–
2 Frances (Fanny) HOLDAWAY 1827–
+William HOPKINS 1828–
3 Jesse HOPKINS 1849–
3 Fanny HOPKINS 1852–1853
3 Sarah Ann HOPKINS 1853–
3 Frederick Robert HOPKINS 1856–
+Sarah Ann 1862–
3 Daniel HOPKINS 1858–
3 William HOPKINS 1860–
3 Thomas HOPKINS 1862–1862
3 James HOPKINS 1863–
3 John HOPKINS 1865–1873
3 Henry HOPKINS 1867–
3 Elizabeth HOPKINS 1868–
3 George HOPKINS 1872–
2 Elizabeth Mary HOLDAWAY 1829–
+Richard George PENSON
3 Seymour Richard George PENSON 1851–
3 Alice Elizabeth PENSON 1853–
3 George Arthur PENSON 1861–1861
3 Maria Amelia PENSON 1863–

Further descendants of Sarah FREEMAN

+Eli NEWMAN 1799–1878 (2nd Husband)
2 Emma Lavinia NEWMAN 1846–1923
+James ALLEN 1826–1915
3 Frank ALLEN 1870–
3 Amy Lavinia ALLEN 1873–
3 Ida Mary Jane ALLEN 1875–
3 Emily Beatrice May ALLEN 1885–1910

Henry James (c.1792– at least 1837)

From convict indent:—
Age 38: brazier, tinman, knife-grinder, soldier. Native of Hampshire, 'abode unknown, not from Headley.' Height 5ft 11½ ins – dark ruddy complexion, black hair going grey, grey eyes, two scars between eyebrows, scar at upper part of left cheek. Could read and write. A widower with children: four boys and three girls (ages unknown).

Warrant dated 2nd December 1830: Machine breaking, riotous assembly and destruction of Headley Union. No former convictions. Sentence: Death, commuted to life transportation. Received on hulk *York* 5th February 1831, sailed on *Eleanor*.

In Australia, he was assigned to Alexander Fraser of Castlereagh and Penrith on the Nepean River, about 35 miles inland from Sydney.

Here was an example of one ex-convict becoming master of another. Fraser had been a clerk in Edinburgh, convicted of fraud in 1817 and transported for seven years, arriving in Australia in 1818. His master, Henry Fulton, had petitioned in 1821 for a mitigation of his sentence, saying "he is a man of considerable abilities as an English teacher, unassuming in his manners, and his behaviour has been exemplary." He later married Fulton's daughter, became the first postmaster of Penrith in 1828, and by 1831 had received a grant of sixty acres from the Governor to add to the 110 acres he already owned.

As to Henry James, perhaps he drew some comfort from seeing how another convict could become reputable so quickly. He was still working for Fraser in Penrith at the time of the 1837 Muster, and his conditional pardon was issued on 9th November 1837—but other than that, as yet we know nothing more about him or his life in Australia.

James Sources: *Jill Chambers, Geof Watts*

John Kingshott (1795–1866)

From convict indent:—

Age 36: farm labourer, of Greatham. Height 5ft 4¼ ins, dark complexion, black hair, grey eyes. Could read. Married. Warrant dated 15th December 1830: Charged with having, on the 23rd day of November last, at the parish of Kingsley, feloniously robbed Mary King of certain loaves of bread, some cheese and beer. Sentence: Death, commuted to life transportation. Conduct record states the offence as 'Machine breaking'. Received on the hulk *York* 9th February 1831, sailed on *Proteus*.

His description as filed in Tasmania adds other personal information: head, round; visage, oval; forehead, perpendicular; whiskers, black; eyebrows, brown; nose, medium length; mouth, wide thick lips; chin, medium length fleshy underneath; arms, hairy.

It is said that he was the second wealthiest man on the *Proteus*, having £10.10s, which in those days was enough to have bought him a passage home had the law allowed it.

He was born around 1795 in Greatham, one of six children of William and Lydia Kingshott, and married Mary Small at Bramshott in 1821. They had five children before the riot (ages in 1830): William (10), Mary Ann (7), Hannah (4), John (2) and Francis (under 1 year).

In Tasmania, John was at first assigned to John Kingstall, but by 1833 was working for a hotelier in New Norfolk, Mrs Ann Bridger, as a farm labourer learning the trade of blacksmith, and an application was made to the authorities for his wife and children to join him.

This was received in England, and on 16th April 1833 the Rev George Godbold of Greatham replied recommending the transfer. Unfortunately, he sent it to Norfolk Island, a thousand miles away in the Pacific Ocean, instead of to New Norfolk in Tasmania(!) and as a result it took a year and a day to reach its intended destination.

By 13th June 1834, an official request had been sanctioned, and in June 1835 the family finally boarded the *Hector* to arrive at Hobart on 20 October.

John and Mary had a sixth child, Ellen, born in New Norfolk on 21st January 1837. Mary died two years later, being buried on 1st March 1839.

John's conditional pardon had been granted, dated 5th April 1838, and in the 1848 census he is shown as the proprietor and person in charge of an unfinished wooden house at Brushy Bottom, New Norfolk employing one ticket-of-leave farm servant. The only other occupant was his daughter Ellen.

The Ship "Hector"

W. Mary Kingshott 33
William Kingshott 16
Mary Kingshott 17
Hannah Kingshott 11
John Henry Kingshott 9
Francis Kingshott 5

being appointed to convey the Persons named in the Margin hereof to Van Diemens Land — they are desired to be on board the said Ship, which is lying at Woolwich, on or before Saturday the 30.th Ins.^t, if their Health should be such as to allow of their undertaking the Voyage: They must be cleanly, and properly clothed, and provided with additional Articles of Wearing Apparel for the Voyage.

Care of Mr Ja.^s Fielder Greatham Petersfield

Authority for John Kingshott's family to join him in Tasmania, then known as Van Diemen's Land

Of his six children, all married, and all but John stayed in Tasmania—the latter followed his father's trade as a blacksmith, moving to Melbourne in 1846, then to the gold diggings near Castlemaine where he seems to have had some success.

John Kingshott of Greatham died on 8th May 1866, age stated as 76 years, a farmer at O'Brien's Bridge, Tasmania. Informant of death was his granddaughter Mary Ann 'Kinshott', the oldest child of his son, William Kingshott.
We are in contact with his descendants both in Victoria and Tasmania.

Kingshott Sources: *Alan Kingshott, Jim Kingshott, John Kingshott, Molly Kingshott, Ann Knight, Geoff Sharman and others*

John Newland (1791–1868)
— the 'Trumpeter' of Selborne —

Age 39: farm labourer, of Adams Lane, Selborne. Warrant dated 29th November 1830: Compelling the Rev Mr Cobbold to sign an agreement to take £300 in lieu of tithe, being much less than the value. Sentence: six months hard labour.

The noted naturalist W. H. Hudson, in his *Hampshire Days*, tells us that the Selborne mob was led by horn-blower, John Newland. He based this largely on talks he had had with Newland's youngest daughters at the beginning of the 20th century, when they were both elderly ladies. They were not even born at the time of the riot, yet the legend of their father's action that day had clearly been passed down to them.

Hudson recorded it as fact, and the village perpetuates the legend, yet several of the things he states are clearly at odds with documentary evidence—a warning to all of us that, however venerable the author, facts should always be checked before one assumes them to be true!

John was born in Selborne on 2nd December 1791, the son of John and Hannah Newlin *(sic)*.

He was enlisted into the army on 1st April 1813, being discharged on 14th December 1819 due to 'Debility caused by disease and wounds when on service with the 2nd Battalion 37th Foot in Holland in action with the enemy.' According to the Regiment's surgeon, he 'received the wound as stated in the body of the discharge in action with the enemy at Bergen op Zoom in 1814.'

He married Ann (née Evans) at Selborne on 13th February 1821, and was her second husband—she had previously married George Kemp and had two children by him (ages in 1830): William (12) and Mary (11). George was buried at Selborne on 24th October 1820.

Ann then had nine children by John—six of them before the riot (ages in 1830): Frederick (9), John (7), Jane (5), Ellen (4), Arthur (2), William baptised 21st May 1830—and three afterwards: James baptised 9 April 1832, Eliza baptised 22nd February 1834, and Harriet baptised 24th June 1838.

In the 1841 Census of Selborne, the Newland family are referred to as 'Paupers'.

Eliza married John Garnett—she was the 'widow Garnett' interviewed by WH Hudson in October 1902. Harriet married James Dewey—she was the 'aged landlady' also referred to by Hudson in his *Hampshire Days*.

Although John Newland was not himself transported, his descendants did eventually arrive in the antipodes.

Ellen Newland was sentenced at the Lent Assizes at Winchester on 1st March 1849 to transportation, charged with the attempted murder of her husband Robert Heath 'with arsenic in a pudding.' Her record states: "I left him for 12 months; after returning to him he accused me of living with another man which led me to the offence for which I am now suffering." She travelled out with her baby daughter Mary Ann on board the *St Vincent* to Tasmania in 1850. The baby died soon after they arrived. Ellen married John Ryan (or Roynan) there in September 1851 and had seven more children. She died in 1908.

In 1884, George Newland, son of James, emigrated to Tasmania on board the *Indus*, and his descendants now live in both Australia and New Zealand.

John Newland died in bed aged 77 in 1868, and was buried near the famous Selborne yew tree at the request of Eliza and William. His grave is marked to this day as the 'Trumpeter's Grave'. His widow, Ann, married yet again the following year, when over 70, and eventually died at the age of 86 years.

Wooden post which once marked the 'Trumpeter's grave' (now standing outside Farnham Museum)

From a talk given in October 1996 to a meeting of the Selborne Association, by Jean Vivian, great-great-granddaughter of John Newland.

The first question most people ask me on hearing of my great-great-grandfather's involvement with the Selborne riots is, "why wasn't he transported along with all the other participants?" A very good question. For if, in fact, John Newland had really been the leader and organiser of the mob he would surely have suffered the same fate instead of getting off with a six-month prison sentence.

The answer, of course, is that he was not the leader—not in the accepted sense of the word—but because he had a horn or bugle, most likely kept from his military service, he was persuaded to walk in front of the mob. It must have made the jeering, noisy throng look pretty impressive.

I am sure he felt it the right thing to do at the time, because although he was a hard-working man, he had a large family to keep on very little money. In fact, the Newland family were paupers, most likely supplementing their living on hand-outs. I try to imagine what it must have been like for him after the fuss had all died down. With the other rioters sentenced and transported, how must he have felt then? I have to assume he kept rather quiet about it, and I'll tell you why.

In 1976 a letter appeared in the *Farnham Herald* from a man living in Tasmania asking if there were any of the Newland family still living in the area. My father wrote to him and received an answer almost by return. It turned out that he was a cousin. His father, my father's uncle George, had emigrated to Tasmania, settled well and had a family. Now they wanted to know the family history. Had great uncle George dropped a few hints I wonder?

My father had been born and brought up in Bentley, and so it seemed the obvious place to start until an aunt told us that she thought the family had originally come from Selborne. Now, to be honest, I had only the vaguest idea where Selborne was, in spite of the fact that we had lived in Blackmoor when I was a child.

My parents, sister and I came to Selborne one day hoping the vicar would have the parish records to hand, but no such luck—they were by this time all at the Hampshire Record Office at Winchester. While we were here in the village, though, we decided to visit the museum in the *Wakes* and found a reference to a John Newland, 'The Trumpeter,' allegedly the leader of the Selborne riots. Could this man be one of our ancestors, we wondered?

My father was cautious, but a visit to the Record Office confirmed the line from John Newland through his son James to his son Frederick, my father's father. Now we knew the connection, but nothing more. And that was how it stayed for a while.

My father died two years later, my mother's health declined, and sadly the correspondence with Tasmania petered out. Nothing more happened until 1993 when over lunch one day some colleagues and I were discussing our family backgrounds. Of course I proudly mentioned my link to Selborne and then, only a few days later, one of the ladies brought me in a copy of an Alton newspaper which had an article about someone having written a book—and play—about the Selborne riots.

Well, this sounded interesting so I rang and booked a couple of seats for the play, *This Bloody Crew*. What a revelation. The myth of the 'Trumpeter' was exposed, but the story was fascinating nonetheless. And it was a strange feeling seeing your ancestors playing out events before your eyes!

After I met Jean as a result of her visit to the play, she joined my writers circle and started work on her fictionalised account of her family history.
The result, 'Echoes of a Trumpet', was published in 1998.

John Owen Smith

James Newland (1832–1901), fourth son of John

Newland Sources: *Jill Chambers, Marian McColl, Nigel Newland, Jean Vivian*

Descendants of John NEWLAND

1 **John NEWLAND 1791–1868**
+Ann EVANS 1795–1881
  2 Frederick NEWLAND 1821–1867
  2 John NEWLAND 1823–
  2 Jane NEWLAND 1825–1864
  2 Ellen NEWLAND 1826–1908
  +Robert HEATH 1794–
    3 Mary Ann HEATH 1849–1850
  *2nd Husband of Ellen NEWLAND:
  +John RYAN
    3 Female RYAN 1852–1852
    3 Female RYAN 1853–
    3 Male RYAN 1855–
    3 William RYAN 1857–1877
    3 John Thomas RYAN 1859–
    3 Male RYAN 1865–
    3 Female RYAN 1870–
  2 Arthur NEWLAND 1828–1857
  2 William NEWLAND 1830–
  +Mary ???
  2 James NEWLAND 1832–1901
  +Mary Ann KNIGHT
    3 James NEWLAND 1858–1858
    3 Frederick NEWLAND 1860–1939
    +Caroline COLES
      4 Frederick NEWLAND 1885–
      +Isabell GANT
      4 Florence NEWLAND 1886–
      +Ernest DEWEY
      4 James NEWLAND 1892–1978
      +Rose BREWER
      4 Joseph NEWLAND 1893–
      4 Owen NEWLAND 1896–1897
      4 Thomas NEWLAND
      4 Rosalie NEWLAND 1898–1966
      4 Eva NEWLAND 1900–1992
      4 Arthur NEWLAND 1901–1979
      +Dorothy Laura TRIBE
        5 Jean Anne NEWLAND 1940–
        5 Beryl Elizabeth NEWLAND 1946–
      4 Robert NEWLAND 1904–1964
      +Margery PAICE
        5 Margery NEWLAND 1938–
      4 Percy NEWLAND 1906–2000
    3 Benjamin NEWLAND 1860–

    3 George NEWLAND 1865–1937
    +Annie RAMPTON
      4 Arthur William NEWLAND 1890–
      +Myrtle SCOTT
        5 Ronald NEWLAND
        +Nellie NORMAN
        5 Gladys NEWLAND
        +Harold GODBER
        5 Jim NEWLAND
        +Margaret JEFFERS
        5 June NEWLAND
        +Alex LOBBAN
        *2nd Husband of June NEWLAND:
        +Newman JONES
      4 Ethel Mary NEWLAND 1892–
      +Richard NICHOLAS
        5 Roy NICHOLAS
        +Nancy RICKLIFF
        5 Margery NICHOLAS
        +Doug MALKIN
      4 George Stanley NEWLAND 1902–1981
      +Mona JACOBSON
        5 Peggy NEWLAND
        +R TWINING
        *2nd Husband of Peggy NEWLAND:
        +Lee BEZZANT
        5 Beverleen NEWLAND
        +Dean DOLAN
        5 Trevor NEWLAND
        +Bernice CROCKER
        5 Patricia NEWLAND
        +Geoff HARGRAVE
        5 Nigel NEWLAND
        +Jenny SHERLOCK
        5 Sonia NEWLAND
        +Scott McCORD
        5 Wendy NEWLAND
        +Leicester SCOTT
    3 Thomas NEWLAND 1869–1897
  2 Eliza NEWLAND 1834–1913
  +John GARNETT 1829–
    3 John GARNETT 1856–
    3 Albert James GARNETT 1854–
    3 Emma Jane GARNETT 1859–
    3 Alfred GARNETT 1862–
    3 Solomon GARNETT 1864–1944
    +Lydia –1945
      4 Albert GARNETT 1890–
      4 Henry GARNETT 1893–
      4 Dorothy GARNETT 1899–
    3 Lily GARNETT 1867–
  2 Harriet NEWLAND 1838–
  +James DEWEY
    3 Alice DEWEY 1877–
    3 Florence DEWEY 1884–

James Painter (1793–1860)

From convict indent:—
Age 36: a farm labourer, of Kingsley parish. Married. Warrant dated 2nd December 1830: Riotous assembly and destruction of Headley Union. No former convictions. Sentence: Death commuted to 7 years transportation.

He was received on the hulk *York* 10th February 1831, and transferred to the hulk *Hardy* on 1st March 1831. For reasons which are not clear, he was never transported, and was granted a free pardon in May 1833. He returned to his family in Kingsley.

James was baptised on 24th March 1793 at Kingsley, the son of Mary (no other information). He married Jane (surname unknown) and they had one child before the riot: Lucy, baptised 18th August 1829 at Kingsley.

Two further children were born after 1830: George (baptised 10th August 1834) and William (baptised 10th October 1841).

The family appears in the 1851 census for Kingsley: James (59), Jane (47), George (16), William (9).

James Painter died in May 1860, stated aged 69, and his wife Mary in 1874 aged 71, both in Kingsley.

Of their sons, George eventually went to Guildford as a blacksmith; William married Sarah Ann Collins in 1863 and went to the Midlands as a shepherd in 1874/75; he died in 1923 at Melton Mowbray.

Painter Sources: Jill Chambers, Lynn Croucher, Graham Harrison

Matthew Triggs (1792–1853)

From convict indent:—
Age stated as 37 (actually 38): a bricklayer for 20 years, of Hollywater, Headley parish. Height 5ft 5¼ ins – ruddy complexion, brown hair, hazel eyes, nose inclined to left, diagonal scar on left eyebrow. Married. Could read but not write. Warrant dated 4th December 1830: Riotous assembly and destruction of Headley Union. No former convictions. Sentence: Death, commuted to life transportation. Received on the hulk *York* 5th February 1831, sailed on *Eleanor*.

Born in Hollywater, a hamlet of Headley, the seventh and youngest child of William and Hannah Triggs, and baptised on 23rd September 1792, Matthew married Mary Croucher at Headley on 30th August 1820. They had five children (ages in 1830): William (9), John (7), Hannah (5), Jane (3) and Sarah (6 months), all born in Headley.

In Australia, Matthew worked first for William Harper at *Oswald* near Greta on the Hunter River, upstream from Maitland.

William Harper, a Scottish surveyor, had arrived in Australia in 1820, bringing with him his newly-purchased theodolite, a rarity which was welcomed by the officials in Sydney. He was appointed assistant-surveyor, and worked for some years surveying many parts of New South Wales. However, by 1826 the wear and tear of this life had taken its toll on him—he had suffered paralysis, lost his sight, and was retired early from duty in 1827.

A broken man, he retreated to *Oswald*, the 2,000-acre estate which he had been granted some years earlier. Here, in 1830, he began to erect a 'comfortable residence' for himself and his family, and he asked the Governor of the day for the assignment of some convicts with skills to assist him—including a brickmaker. Whether or not this request resulted in Matthew Triggs being assigned to him the following year, we can only guess.

There were stories of Harper being a cruel landowner, but this has never been proved. He died in May 1836 aged 44 years, and was buried on his own property at a place now known locally as 'Harpers Hill'.

Matthew then worked for Harper's wife, Catherine, at Maitland, and was granted his conditional pardon on 9th November 1837. Maitland at this time had a brickworks and was becoming a prosperous area, with demands for his skills as a bricklayer.

He died on 30th November 1853 in Maitland Hospital aged 61 years, and is buried in Grave 33 at Camp Hill Cemetery, West Maitland. Interestingly, there is another Triggs laid to rest nearby—Joseph, who died two years later in 1855 aged 40 years. So far we have been unable to establish any connection between the two.

From a talk given in October 1996 to a meeting of the Selborne Association, by Ann, wife of Philip Viney, the great-great-grandson of Matthew Triggs.

We began searching into our family history in 1986 and found Matthew's wife Mary and the children on the various census records, but no trace of Matthew at all; we searched the burial records but still could not find out what had happened to him—a complete mystery. Then a year later we saw a small book produced by the local WI on Headley Grange, the old workhouse, and there, jumping out of the page, was Matthew Triggs' name—we had found him at last—to us it was a little bit like striking gold.

When Matthew was transported, he left behind his wife Mary, just 30 years old, and five children ranging in age from 10 years to just a few months old. It must have been a struggle, but somehow they survived and grew to maturity. Four of them married, but William, the eldest, joined the Navy and 'died in war'.

Mary Triggs and the family continued to live in Hollywater after Matthew was transported, at the home of Jane Tuckey who was the grandmother of Mary and owned the cottage. Matthew's youngest child was Sarah, and she remembered having to get up early in the mornings to make sure the old lady did not fall and hurt herself. The family lived there until Jane died in 1840, aged 90, when the cottage was sold to Andrew Warren and the money shared among the family.

The family then moved, staying within Headley parish. At the age of 12½, Sarah had an illegitimate son, Henry James, who it seems was claimed by her mother Mary, baptised as her son and brought up by her. One more mouth to feed.

Sarah took up dressmaking, and at age 19 she married James Upperton, a Headley shoemaker and grocer. By 1871, Sarah & James were living at the *Crown Inn*, Arford—James was innkeeper and also still a grocer. It was about this time that Mary moved into the *Crown Inn*, and it was there she died of dropsy in August 1876. She was 72, had lived to see four of her children married and had at least 15 grandchildren. Although she probably had no way of knowing it, she survived Matthew by 23 years.

Triggs Sources: *Jill Chambers, Philip & Ann Viney, Geof Watts*

Matthew's granddaughter Emmeline
with husband John Henry Viney about 1880

Descendants of Matthew TRIGGS

1 **Matthew TRIGGS 1792–1853**
+Mary CROUCHER 1805–1876
2 William TRIGGS 1820–
2 John TRIGGS 1823–1887
  +Ann LANGFORD 1824–1893
  3 William TRIGGS 1846–1928
    +Matilda MOSS 1849–1897
  3 James John TRIGGS 1850–1919
    +Emily HORLOCK 1850–1912
    4 William Langford TRIGGS 1879–1956
      +Maude RUSSEN 1880–1936
      5 Claude William TRIGGS 1911–
        +Rita MOFFATT 1911–
      5 Joyce Maud TRIGGS 1917–
        +Jack FORWOOD
  3 Clara Kate Elizabeth TRIGGS 1852–1935
    +Dick HALL 1863–1931
  3 Eva TRIGGS 1855–
    +Capt GULLY (not married)
    4 Daughter TRIGGS 1876–
    4 Gordon TRIGGS 1887–
  3 Emmeline TRIGGS 1858–1939
    +John Henry VINEY 1857–1928
    4 Frank Augustus VINEY 1880–1945
    +Ellen ROWE
    4 Percy Gilbert VINEY 1881–1916
    4 Mildred Kate VINEY 1884–1900
    4 Janetta Adelaide VINEY 1886–1955
    4 Elsie Winifred VINEY 1889–
    4 Robert Alexander VINEY 1893–1960
    4 Adrian Cecil VINEY 1896–1955
      +Lillian Maria TILBURY 1901–1991
      5 Jean Ann VINEY 1922–1977
      5 Rita Mavis Ruth VINEY 1924–
      5 Iris Mildred Clare VINEY 1926–
      5 Vaughan Richard John VINEY 1927–1929
      5 Pendrick Cecil Ralph VINEY 1932–
      5 Philip Wilfred VINEY 1934–
        +Ann WHITEHEAD 1934–
      5 Hilary Lillian VINEY 1938–

2 Hannah TRIGGS 1825–1883
  +Abraham GAUNTLETT 1819–1866
  3 George GAUNTLETT 1845–
  3 Jane GAUNTLETT 1847–1922
  3 Mary Ann GAUNTLETT 1849–1876
  3 William GAUNTLETT 1851–
  3 James GAUNTLETT 1854–
  3 Walter GAUNTLETT 1856–
  3 Harriet GAUNTLETT 1860–
    +Frederick GAUNTLETT 1863–1925
    4 Winifred M GAUNTLETT 1889–
    4 Lilian M GAUNTLETT 1890–
    4 Daisy Olive GAUNTLETT 1891–
    4 Jessie GAUNTLETT 1892–1918
    4 Harry Frederick GAUNTLETT 1897–
  3 Thomas GAUNTLETT 1863–
  3 Eva Eliza GAUNTLETT 1866–
  *2nd Husband of Hannah TRIGGS:
  +??? ROE
2 Jane TRIGGS 1827–
  +Charles GODDARD –1860
  *2nd Husband of Jane TRIGGS:
  +Charles OSBORNE
2 Sarah TRIGGS 1830–1898
  +D BERRY (not married)
  3 Henry James TRIGGS 1842–
  *1st Husband of Sarah TRIGGS:
  +James UPPERTON 1827–1891

98

Other Rioters

Robert Bennett – age 16. Warrant dated 15th December 1830 relating to Selborne workhouse – acquitted.

William Bicknell – age 23. Warrant dated 26th November 1830 relating to Headley workhouse – acquitted.

Henry Bone – age 31. Warrant dated 4th December 1830 relating to Selborne workhouse – one year with hard labour.

William Bright – age 22. Warrant dated 2nd December 1830: Charged with having, on the 24th day of November last, at the parish of Headley, feloniously robbed Ann Parker of one shilling and one half crown, the current coin of the realm, the monies of Robert Parker. Acquitted.

John Cobb – age 27 of Selborne. Warrant dated 4th December 1830 relating to Selborne workhouse – two years with hard labour.

Thomas Hoare – age 36 of Selborne. Warrant dated 2nd December 1830 relating to Selborne workhouse – two years hard labour.

William Hoare – age 39 of Selborne. Warrant dated 14th December 1830 relating to Selborne workhouse – two years hard labour.

Thomas Marshall – age 21. Warrant dated 26th November 1830: Charged with having, on the 23rd day of November instant, at the parish of Headley, riotously assembled together, and feloniously, with force, demolished the poor house of the united parishes of Bramshott, Headley and Kingsley, situated in the parish of Headley, and pulled the same down. Stands further charged with having feloniously robbed one widow King of a large quantity of bread, cheese, and beer, the goods and chattels of the said widow King and William King. Sentence: Death, commuted to one year with hard labour.

Thomas Robinson – age 67 of Empshott? Warrant dated 26th November 1830 relating to Headley workhouse. Rev Charles Alcock of Empshott referred to him as being "deeply concerned in the outrage in Headley, and will never see the country more, if he does not suffer the worst." He was acquitted!

Benjamin Smith – age 23 of Selborne. Warrant dated 15th December 1830 relating to Selborne workhouse – 6 months with hard labour.

John Trimming – age 25 of Selborne. Warrant dated 6th December 1830 relating to mobbing the vicar – one year with hard labour.

The Clergymen

Rev Robert Dickinson (1769–1847)

Age 61: born 12th August 1769 at Lyth, Westmoreland; Queen's College, Oxford: matriculated 1786 (aged 16), BA 1791, MA 1795, Fellow and tutor; Rector of Headley 1818–47; died 1st November 1847 at Cheshunt, Herts.

According to *Headley 1066–1966* by Canon Tudor Jones, Mr Dickinson was 'a great deal non-resident, and suffered from ill-health, though he was described as "a jolly big old farmer."'

All Saints' Church, Headley, with a spire before 1836

Rev William Rust Cobbold (1773–1841)

Age 57: born at Wilby, Suffolk, son of Thomas, clergyman; matriculated at Trinity College, Oxford in 1792 (aged 19); Magdalen College, Oxford – BA 1794, MA 1797, BD 1805; Fellow and tutor; Vicar of Selborne 1813–41; died 19th August 1841 at Ludgate Hill, London; buried at Kensal Green.

Mr GV Cox, chorister of Magdalen College in 1793, speaks of Cobbold as the College Schoolmaster in the following terms:—

"Having during one or two of his last years been a pupil of Mr Cobbold, I am entitled to speak of the impressions left upon me by his teaching: they are these – that from a bilious constitution, betrayed by his yellow-tinted complexion, he was ill-qualified to bear kindly and patiently with little ignorant boys. 'Alphezibeus, Sir,' he would say; 'don't you know s from z? Listen, Sir, Al-phe-si-be-us;' every syllable, especially the third, being impressed by a sharp cut with a cane, or a sharper twitch of an ear. Indeed this latter punishment, his favourite one, extended several times to the partial tearing the ear from the head of a dull boy!"

The conflicts between Cobbold and his parishioners for several years before the riot of 1830 are well documented, a particularly interesting account coming from his own pen in a document entitled *Abuse of the Poor Laws in the Parish of Selborne, Hants*. This document, which came to light in 1946, has been summarised by Mr L Sunderland, himself a vicar of Selborne, in his booklet *Trouble at Selborne*, published in 1967.

Even after the riots, Mr Cobbold seems to have shown no sense of amelioration towards his flock. In a letter from him appended to the Second Annual Report of the Poor Law Commissioners in 1836, he writes:—

"It is to the operation of this Act entirely (Poor law Amendment Act 1834) by withholding from the labourer the means of frequenting the public houses and beer shops, that I attribute the present peace and quiet of the streets as compared with what it used to be. I consider the Poor Law Amendment Act one of the greatest blessings which could have been conferred on a parish like Selborne and I do not despair now of seeing the rude people of this place become perfectly civilized and of a very different character to what they have hitherto been."

Cobbold's death in a road traffic accident was reported in the *Gentleman's Magazine* of November 1841 as follows:—

"Died at the Belle Sauvage, Ludgate Hill, aged 68, the Rev. William Rust Cobbold, Rector (sic) of Selborne, Hants.

The death of this gentleman was occasioned by his being knocked down, six days before, by the Oxford Mail cart at the end of Ludgate Hill. Being a very corpulent man, it was two days before it was discovered that his ribs were broken. A Coroner's jury returned a verdict of accidental death, accompanied by a censure on the Surgeon, who had not paid the case sufficient attention."

Magdalen College recorded the same event in Latin:—

A.D. 1841. Aug. *"Circiter hoc tempus casus funestus e vivis aufert Gulielmum Rust Cobbold, S.T.B. nostri Collegii olim Socium, et Vicarium de Selborne in comitatu Hanton.*

Quum enim ad Londinium se contulisset, negotii obeundi causa, et per vias omni rhedarum genere refertas gradu titubanti, quippe qui annis provectus et corpore infirmus, festinaret, a curru temere acto eversus fuit, et in talem modum sauciatus, ut post paucos dies animam apud diversorium, ubi commoratus est, expiravit." V.P. Reg.

William Cowburn

William Cowburn Esq, aged 48 in 1830, was a London lawyer resident in Selborne at the time of the riot who, while deploring the outbreak, strove energetically to obtain a reprieve from the gallows for Robert Holdaway. The son of James Cowburn, a Lancashire man who became bankrupt, he married Catherine Smith of Camer in 1816.

The Cowburns rented a property 'with a lawn' in the centre of Selborne from Miss Mary White (this may have been *Wakes*, which we know she inherited) and left the village in 1832, moving to Sydenham, Kent. William Cowburn died in 1854.

Early in 1830, before the riot occurred, he had published an 'address' to the 'Cottagers of Selborne' recommending ways in which they might use a bit of 'self-help' to improve their lot:—

COTTAGERS OF SELBORNE

I have been induced to draw up the following statement of facts, that the Cottagers of Selborne may see the many advantages to be derived from industry.

In Yorkshire, a poor man of the name of Thomas Rook, rented a small portion of land, and the only persons he had to assist him were his wife and a girl of twelve years of age; the only time he could work himself were the leisure hours after his daily labor was over. His family lived well, never applied to the parish for relief, and he has been enabled to lay by a sufficient sum to place out his two sons, and to furnish them with clothes and other necessaries.

In 1802, another poor man of the same neighbourhood rented one acre and a quarter of land; before he entered upon the occupation he had the greatest difficulty in maintaining his wife and three children, for he had no land, and was therefore obliged to buy every article of food. In 1809 his family had increased to seven children, yet, though from frequent ill health he had not been able to earn the high wages obtained by many of his fellow-laborers, he supported his family without any parochial relief.

These two instances furnish sufficient proof of the vast benefit that must arise to laborers from being enabled to cultivate a portion of land for themselves. Much time which otherwise would necessarily be spent in idleness, after the daily work is over, may, by this means, be advantageously and pleasantly employed; and not only that, but it furnishes full employment to the wives of the cottagers, and gives the children early habits of industry.

It may be asked, how the Cottager can make the cultivation of land furnish him with means of subsistence, when he hears that the farmer is much troubled to make it answer. But this difficulty can be easily and satisfactorily answered. The farmer incurs great expense by the men he employs, but the poor man only employs his idle time; he works himself, and enjoys the produce of his own labors, always feeling that independence will be the reward of his labors; and who that is born in a free country would not glory in such an idea; would not, while he is exerting his strength, delight in the thought that he will no longer be obliged to apply to the parish to assist him in supporting himself and his family?

The answer of a poor man in a parish in Berkshire, who enjoyed the benefit of renting a small piece of land, is well worth remembering; he was asked, he was even solicited, by the parish officers, to accept of some assistance for the support of his nine children. His reply was, on no account; I keep my family, thank God, very well, and would, on no consideration, be beholden to the parish.

I have one more instance to bring forward, which even exceeds those which have gone before. A laborer at Hasketon, in Suffolk, rented a piece of ground, and died, leaving a widow with fourteen children, the eldest a girl under fourteen. The parish is within the district of the incorporated houses of industry, the directors of which immediately agreed to relieve the poor widow by taking her seven youngest children into the house. This was proposed to her, but, with great agitation of mind, she refused to part with any of her children. She said she would rather die in working to maintain them, or go herself with all of them into the house and work for them there, than part with them, or suffer any partiality to be shewn to any of them. She then declared that if the farmer would continue her as his tenant, she would undertake to maintain and bring up all her family without parochial assistance. She persisted in her resolution, and being a strong woman of about forty-five years of age, her landlord told her she should continue and hold it the first year rent free. This she accepted with much thankfulness, and again assured him she would manage for her family without any other assistance.

She has kept her word, placing out twelve of her children in service, and regularly paying her rent, after the first year. She came at length to her landlord, and informed him that as she had now only her two youngest children left with her, who could, indeed, almost maintain themselves; she had taken to the employment of nurse, which was a less laborious situation; she therefore gave up the land, expressing great gratitude for the enjoyment of it, as it had afforded her the means of supporting her family, under a calamity, which must otherwise have driven both her and her children into a workhouse.

Who, that reads the above, would not earnestly desire to possess the means of rendering himself and family independent of parochial relief? It has been found to answer in various parts of the kingdom, and why should it not meet with success at Selborne, where the peasants possess health, strength, and means sufficient for the undertaking? It is to be hoped that they also possess a spirit of independence equal to what is found in other places, which will induce them to labor for themselves, rather than be dependent on parish assistance.

Your well wisher,
W. COWBURN.
LONDON, February, 1830.

Following the riot, he was asked by a local MP to write an account of the conduct of the mob at Selborne. This was sent, with other documents, as an affidavit in favour of Holdaway to Lord Melbourne and Baron Vaughan:—

In the latter end of November 1830 the Laborers and poor of Selborne in Hampshire required an increase in wages, and that the Governor of the workhouse should be discharged. The wages were deemed to be too small, and the Governor oppressive. The maximum of wages there has been 9/- a week for able laborers, less for young men, boys, and women, and some men not being strong only 1/- a day, or 6/- a week. The parish allowance to parish laborers working on the roads was 10d a day. This must be admitted to be on too low a scale. The wages demanded was 2/- a day, which cannot be deemed too much.

The Farmers deliberated, but came to no decision. The Laborers then invited the surrounding parishes to join them, and formed a mob of from 300 to 500 which increased to 800 or 900. They then required the Farmers to attend the vicar (the Rev Wm Cobbold) and demanded of the latter that he should reduce his Tithes, and of all of them that wages should be increased, and the Governor of the workhouse discharged. Some reluctancy was shown, and they proceeded to the workhouse, destroyed the furniture, and broke the windows.

They then returned to the vicar and allowed him just half an hour and, that expired, 5 minutes to decide, when a rush was about to take place upon him and his house, and to save his life and property he came out and signed the paper prepared for him agreeing to accept £300 a year in lieu of taking in kind of from 600 to 900 a year. The remainder of this night was past in eating, drinking and rioting, and the following morning their banner was again displayed, their force called together by the sound of horns, and compelling all laborers every where to join, they accumulated it is said 1,100 and proceeded to Headley, a neighbouring parish, and did as at Selborne.

Money was asked for and given at Selborne, and was spent in eating and drinking. The poor of Selborne, if not oppressed, have at least not been sufficiently attended to, the laborers not sufficiently rewarded, and in many instances throughout the county similar causes have produced similar effects. The following instance may tend to illustrate that, where the poor are attended to, they can feel gratitude and abstain from doing mischief.

A family[†] have resided at Selborne about half of each year for the last 8 or 9 years. They have been uniformly, but only ordinarily attentive to the poor, and have not been overnice in selecting the worthy only, but by employing and relieving occasionally some of an opposite character, as it was said have tried to reclaim them. Early this year an address was circulated by this family among the laborers to encourage industry; and land was granted to any poor man who desired it of an acre or two to each, to enable them to grow their own potatoes, and wheat for bread.

When the mob assembled, though collected from almost all the surrounding parishes, it seems to have been a well understood rule among them that they were not to injure any thing belonging to this family nor at all to annoy them, and this was carried so far that although the Man Servant, when numbers were collected about the gate, asked them what they wanted, or what they would have, the immediate answer was "nothing here, this gentleman and lady bear too good characters and are too good to the poor, and we will not hurt a stick or stone about them", nor did they.

On another occasion when they came and forced away the Outdoor Servant, they told a woman servant not to let her mistress be alarmed for they would not injure any thing, but the labouring man they must have to join them. And they were overheard to say in different parts of the mob that nothing must be injured about this family. In the evening, some stragglers came down and asked for something to eat and drink, and when they returned and told the main body it was the cause of a quarrel, and some say of a fight, at all events great displeasure was expressed that this family had been disturbed at all.

The lady was at this time alone with a numerous family, so that the power of causing terror, doing mischief, and exciting any thing was very great. It is also the more remarkable because this is almost the only assailable family at this beautiful sequestered spot, for which even Cobbett says "God has done everything."

A few nights afterwards a house was set on fire, and the gentleman of this family (for he was soon there) can bear ample testimony to the readiness with which his orders and advice were attended, which it is

---

[†] Cowburn was referring to his own family here.

106

*believed by the nearest Magistrate and other Gentlemen, prevented the
fire spreading and saved great part of this village.*

*For some years the Farmers have been distressed and the poor
laws have borne heavily upon them, and to relieve themselves they
have naturally kept wages as low, and the relief to the poor as low too,
as they possibly could so that the laborers and poor have suffered
beyond human bearing and now comes the reaction. This should be
remedied, but <u>how</u>. Let statesmen judge.*

And finally, we have an account of the riot and trials from James Bridger,
one of the more significant farmers of Selborne parish, written soon after the
events at the request of William Cowburn:—

*To: Wm Cowburn Esq
    14 Tavistock Sq
    London*

                                              Selborne, Jany 12th 1831

Sir,

*I hear from T. Hoare it is your wish to have an account from us
respecting the proceedings at Selborne on the 22 Nov, which I now
give to the best of my recollection.*

*We did not hear until the morning of the 21st that there would be a
mob at Selborne, and then Mr Hale [a Farmer] and Mr Collyer
[Church Warden] went to Mr Cobbold to request his advice. He was
very short with them and told them they might do as they thought
proper, for his part he could do nothing.*

*We had heard of Riots in many places round us, and certainly
expected it here, to prevent which we called a meeting a few days
before and agreed to advance the labourers wages to 2/- a day, which
we thought would prevent any thing of the sort here. According to the
report of the Times, Mr C accuses us of inciting the labourers to make
the demand on him, which is very false as on the contrary we did every
thing in our power to prevent them breaking in at his gate, of which we
have plenty of witnesses, and that I told him when he asked us if we
should consider his agreement binding, that I certainly should not.*

*The 'Times' goes on to state what they consider to be the most
criminal part of the conduct of us Farmers. They say after forcing C.
to sign away his property we distinguished ourselves in defending our
own Property, the Workhouse, but this again is wrong. Whether by
design in C. or by mistatement of the reporter I know not, but the
damage was done to the workhouse before they went to C. There was
an attempt made to save the workhouse, the particulars of which I
believe you know.*

*Mr Debenham Snr, on his arrival at Selborne, asked the people
what they wanted; they said an advance of wages and also to lower the*

Tithe. Mr D. remonstrated with them on its being an unlawful proceeding, when they immediately surrounded him and with uplifted clubs demanded what he meant, which with the treatment his son had received at the workhouse before was enough to convince us that persuasion and not force would be of any avail, and there were only about few of us unarmed against 300.

Mr C. also accuses us of giving them Beer, and ordering it to be charged to the Parish, but here again I think we have reason to complain, as he was the first to propose its being charged to the Parish Acct, and mentioned how much he thought each man should have, and Eade [Church Warden] wished half of the Beer to be had from his House.

There seems to be great odium thrown upon us for signing the paper, although C. was the first to put his name to it, and Eade drew up the agreement and handed it to most of the Farmers for them to sign, and also wrote a copy and gave it to the men and the original to me, and even after my Father had several times refused to sign, held a hat for him to lay the paper on. After C. had signed, the mob declared they would not leave till he had given them five Pounds. We then stepped forward and told them they should have no such thing, we (the Farmers) would sooner join round and give them some ourselves. C. then proposed its being charged to the Parish.

We should have contradicted the statement of C. before, but our attorney, Mr Mellersh of Godalming, wished us to be quiet for a time and not even to let any one know we had had any advice. It is our most anxious wish to have this affair sifted to the bottom, as I think C. will then be seen in his proper colours. We can make it appear we advised the men to abstain from violence, and that if we had not been there the consequences would have been a good deal worse for C. as many of the Labourers are ready to come forward and say. We did every thing in our power to keep them quiet, and when Cobb, one of the most active amongst them, got in at his gate we ordered him out.

I called upon poor Holdaway to do all he could to keep them out. It appears C. knew the intentions of the mob toward him for several hours before any of the Farmers, except those living on the spot, were there. Surely he ought to have requested our assistance, and then if we had refused he would have had a just reason to complain of us. We refused for some time to give any Beer, and only consented at last on condition they should immediately disperse and go to their work.

We had given Mr Harrison [master of the Selborne workhouse] instructions the evening before, in case the labourers should go to him before we were there, to assure them in our names their wages should be raised if they would be peaceable, which we thought would satisfy them, as we had no thoughts of their interfering with Mr C. or of seeing any more than our own parishioners there. We can prove also that on hearing of the disturbances in other places, we had mentioned to the principal Farmer of a neighbouring parish that we should wish to advance the price of labour, in order to prevent similar disturbances here.

I think we should not have had so much blame thrown upon us if E^d. Fitt had not given such miserable evidence. I asked him the other day how he came to say in court he was one of those Farmers who were inciting the mob to make the demand on C., to which he instantly replied, Well, he was in sight of them, how could he help seeing them when they stood right before his eyes.

Perhaps, Sir, you could inform us if it is possible to get a correct statement of C's evidence and if so in what way, as we should then know better how to proceed. For my own part I am determined, if any thing can be done the matter shall not rest as it is. Should you, Sir, think proper to publish any thing from this unconnected statement, all we have to request is it may be done in such a way that we may not appear to be acting contrary to the advice of Messrs Mellersh & Marsham. I should take it as a very great favor if you would return us a line or two upon this subject, and remain

Sir Your Most
   Obedient Servant
      James Bridger

The Rioters' Walk

❧ ❧ ❧

— a guided walk —

from

Selborne to Headley

and back again

Distance approximately 7 miles out and 7 miles back

The walk starts from the *Queens Hotel* (the *Compasses* in 1830) in Selborne going to the *Holly Bush* in Headley by way of Whitehill and Standford, and returning by way of Kingsley and Oakhanger.

Refreshment is available at the start and end points, and also at the *Royal Oak* (Hollywater), *Robin Hood* (Standford), *Cricketers* (Kingsley) and *Red Lion* (Oakhanger).

Note that suggested routes through Military and National Trust land between Whitehill and Standford, while open to walkers at the time of writing, are not marked as public rights of way on maps.

No difficult climbs, but the walk can be very muddy in places.

Recommended map: Ordnance Survey Explorer No. 133

Map of the Rioters' Walk

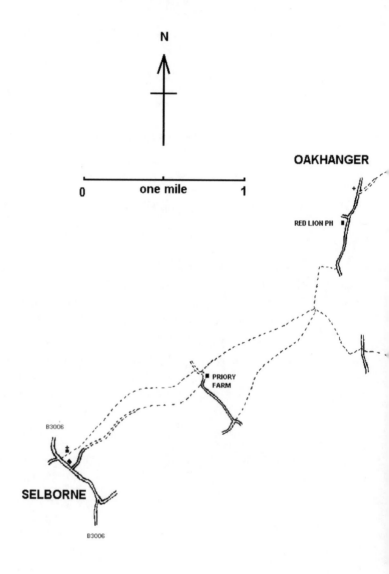

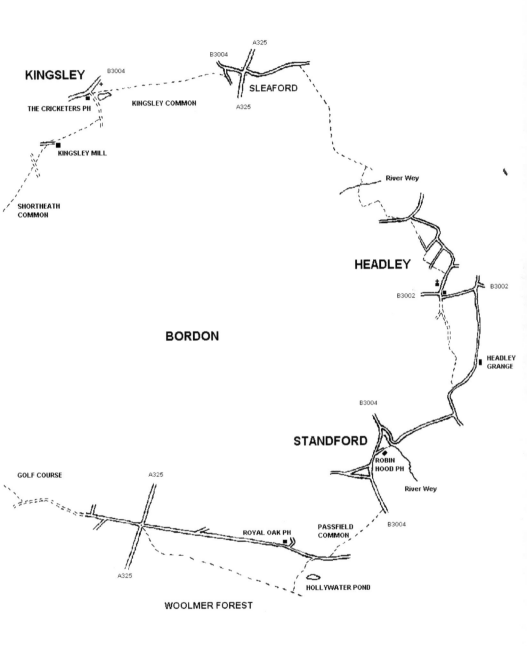

KINGSLEY

B3004

B3004

A325

SLEAFORD

A325

THE CRICKETERS PH

KINGSLEY COMMON

KINGSLEY MILL

River Wey

SHORTHEATH
COMMON

HEADLEY

B3002

B3002

BORDON

HEADLEY
GRANGE

B3004

STANDFORD

ROBIN
HOOD PH

GOLF COURSE

A325

River Wey

PASSFIELD
COMMON

ROYAL OAK PH

B3004

A325

HOLLYWATER POND

WOOLMER FOREST

Selborne to Headley

From the *Queens Hotel*, take Huckers Lane which runs by the side of the hotel garden and drops down to *Dortons*. This becomes a bridleway, muddy in places, above the valley of the Oakhanger Stream through a beech hanger and then across fields. At Priory Farm, turn right up a metalled road to the top of the hill where it meets Honey Lane. From here there is a view over the Oakhanger valley, today noted for its satellite tracking stations.

Take the footpath down through fields towards Oakhanger for about a mile. At the five-way junction of footpaths (which you will also meet on the way back), turn sharp right emerging after about half a mile by the side of Springfields Nurseries. Cross the road here, taking the track almost opposite the Nursery entrance. After crossing the stream take the track to the left of a house. This passes through Blackmoor Golf Course, joining another track known as Eveley Lane before becoming a metalled road.

Follow this road (which soon has a pavement) straight to the roundabout on the main road (A325) at Whitehill—cross here with care.

You now have the choice of following the metalled road (Liphook Road) ahead, or cutting into the Military land of Woolmer Forest just to the right of it. Even when the red flags are flying, it is possible to walk outside the danger zone following close to the course of the old Longmoor Military Railway towards Hollywater.

On this route you pass close beside two distinct hills, or 'clumps', on your left— probably these would have been treeless and therefore more prominent landscape features in 1830.

After about a mile, join the line of the old railway and look for a barrier leading to a grass track on the left, alongside the garden of *Stone Cottage*, which becomes a vehicle access road, crosses the stream from Hollywater Pond, and re-joins Liphook Road opposite Passfield Common (which is National Trust land).

The Common is fenced to allow for stock grazing, but there is a stile to enter it. You will have to discover your own track across—be warned, it is extremely boggy in places. If you are not dressed for walking over very wet ground, you may prefer to take the next entrance into the common, through a gate further up the road beyond the house. Head for the north corner of the common and a stile over the fence about 50 yards from the corner, emerging on the B3004 Liphook to Bordon road at a point where a small rivulet passes under the road, marking the boundary between Bramshott and Headley parishes.

Cross the road and turn left along the verge path, passing both the Methodist Church and Gospel Hall on your left before going downhill to Standford Village Green. Here the *Robin Hood* offers refreshment.

Leave the village green by the small road which leads to a ford across the River Wey. There is a footbridge. Keep straight on at its junction with Tulls Lane, following the metalled road uphill between hedges to a triangular junction at the top. Turn left here, along (another) Liphook Road.

This is the road by which the rioters entered Headley in 1830. The old workhouse (now *Headley Grange*) is about half a mile away on the right hand side—and if you wish, you may walk past it into Headley as the rioters did. However, if you have had enough of walking on roads, take the footpath to the left immediately after the first sharp bend (by an electricity sub-station) and follow it to emerge in the centre of Headley where the *Holly Bush* stands.

Notes on the walk — Selborne to Headley

We don't know for certain which route the rioters took in their march from Selborne to Headley, and it could be that several groups went different ways. The most direct route from the centre of Selborne in those days would probably have been some near-variation of the one we have chosen. However, we are told that Robert Holdaway went to collect signatures from farms near Empshott and Greatham on the way, in which case his route would have been considerably longer.

The communities of Bordon and Whitehill did not exist then, but I was interested to know if the Farnham to Petersfield turnpike (now the A325) had been constructed at that time. If so, it might have formed a convenient route for the marchers to move from Greatham to Whitehill instead of cutting across the uncharted tracks of Woolmer Forest on their way to Hollywater. But I discovered that although the turnpike had received Royal Assent in 1826, it was apparently not completed until 1832.

When William Cobbett rode through Woolmer Forest in his *Rural Ride* of 24th November 1822, he said of it, "The road was not ... without its dangers, the forest being full of quags and quick-sands." He also said of it, "This is a tract of Crown-lands ... on some parts of which our Land Steward, Mr Huskisson, is making some plantations of trees, partly fir, and partly other trees. What he can plant the fir for, God only knows ..."

Close to Hollywater Clump is the spot where the old parishes of Selborne, Headley and Bramshott met, at the chimney of a house which has since been demolished.

The hamlet of Hollywater is still located where three parishes meet—and as such is claimed by no-one and forgotten by most. It has had a reputation in the past of being a place where the people who joined the march described as "forest dwellers and travellers" might well have lived.

Standford was one of the main local centres of industry in 1830, with two paper mills and a corn mill operating on the River Wey. The Warren family, who ran the paper mills there from the 1820s until the early 20th century, were staunch Methodists, and the 'non-conformist' nature of the community is in evidence even now with its Methodist Church and Gospel Hall.

Although paper mills in Buckinghamshire were being attacked by mobs in the very week that 'our' riot occurred, those at Standford were not touched as far as we can tell. Perhaps there was no machinery installed in them at that time, or at least none that could be seen to be causing unemployment. For whatever reason, the mob appears to have passed through Standford, crossed the ford and headed up Tulls Lane towards the workhouse.

The Headley 'House of Industry' had been built in 1795 at an estimated cost of some £1,500 for the parishes of Headley, Bramshott and Kingsley, to shelter their infirm, aged paupers, and orphan or illegitimate children. After the 1830 riot, the building was repaired, and in the 1841, 1851 and 1861 censuses it is shown still being used as a workhouse. It was sold in 1870 to a builder for £420, and he converted it into a private house, now known as *Headley Grange*. In November 1872, he resold the building to Mr Theophilus Sigismund Hahn for £490.

After two further changes in ownership, *Headley Grange* was used during the 1970s as a recording studio, and there, early in 1971, "Out of the clear blue pool of creativity arose the eight-minute extravaganza which would become Led Zeppelin's ultimate trademark, a song of shimmering and flourishing beauty, a supreme accomplishment which Robert Plant would later describe as 'our single most important achievement' ... *Stairway to Heaven*."[‡]

Today the house remains a private residence. On St George's Day 1994, descendants of four of the rioters, along with representatives from Selborne and Headley, assembled in the garden to plant a cutting from the old Selborne Yew in memory of the transportations.

The present *Holly Bush* in Headley High Street is not a building which would have been present in 1830. In fact we believe the old *Holly Bush* to have been situated across the road in the house now called *Wakefords*. William Cobbett mentions visiting here on his Rural Ride of 24th November 1822.

Mr Lickfold's shop is still to be seen, though no longer a shop—it is the building now called *Crabtree House* which faces north along the length of the High Street, with a good view of what was going on there at the time.

[‡] *'Led Zeppelin, the definitive biography,'* by Ritchie Yorke

Headley to Selborne

From the *Holly Bush*, turn right along Headley High Street, past the church and the old rectory, and just before *Belmont* take a path to the left. This crosses a road and then passes along two sides of the Holme School grounds, emerging in Church Lane at a right-angle bend.

Turn left along Church Lane (a cul-de-sac) and at its end pass through a footpath gate and downhill across fields. You emerge by Huntingford Farm, at the junction of Curtis Lane and Frensham Lane. The original route to Trottsford would have gone right and then left here, past Linsted Farm and Headley Wood Farm, but this is now closed as a right of way. Instead, turn left, following Frensham Lane towards Lindford for a short distance, then take the footpath to the right, which follows the road uphill for a while before bearing right and becoming sandy.

After passing through some woodland, this diverted right of way crosses the River Wey by way of an old aqueduct and then zigzags sharply uphill. At its junction with a track at the top of a rise, look back the way you have come—if the trees are not obscuring it, and if you know where to look, you may just make out the top of Headley Church tower nestling among the treetops.

Here you rejoin the original route. Turn left along the track and follow it for just under a mile to Pickett's Hill road. Turn left, and follow the road down to its junction with the main A325 at Sleaford. Here there is a set of traffic lights. Cross the main road diagonally, and follow the nearby side road towards the back of the *New Inn* (now redeveloped), then turn sharp right on the old road which passes over the River Slea.

After crossing the river, take the public track leading off through Army land across Kingsley Common. Note that the route is not as straightforward as the OS map suggests—about 100 yards after crossing the open space by *Coldharbour*, look for a less significant track branching to the right, just past a 'crossroads' of vehicular tracks. Follow this until it passes the pond on the left. Here, in Kingsley village, you will find the *Cricketers* available for refreshment.

To continue the walk, follow the track between the pub car park and the pond, pass Ockham Hall, and shortly turn along the first track on your right past some houses. Follow footpath signs left and right, past the aptly named Meadowgate Farm, over a stile and along a fence across a flat field.

After another footpath joins at a double stile, you pass the garden of Kingsley Mill on your left. Cross a stile and a stone slab bridge over a culvert, and cross the drive of the mill, then follow the footpath diagonally across the orchard and over the mill leat, and round a bend to another stile.

Cross a field and go over a disused railway embankment. From here the original course of the path has been diverted due to sand works. Follow the path round the edge of a field, then cross a stile onto Shortheath Common. Once again, the route is not as straightforward here as the OS map suggests. Keeping all houses to your left, cross one vehicular track, then join another. Go along this track, ignoring turns—it becomes less well-used by vehicles as it continues south-west across the common and into the centre of Oakhanger village. Here, at the village green, turn left along the pavement of the metalled road through the village. The *Red Lion* soon offers refreshment on your right.

Cottage at Oakhanger—footpath passes in front after leaving the road

At the bend in the road as you leave the village, take the footpath to the right, along the garden wall of an old thatched cottage *(see photo above)*. Cross the field, and follow the footpath to the left, arriving at the five-ways junction you met on your outward journey.

You may, of course, return to Selborne by following the outward route in reverse from here. Alternatively, turn right and follow the course of the stream more closely towards Priory Farm. Be warned—this can be tough on the ankles if muddy hoof-prints have hardened! Cross the stream by a footbridge, then cross over a track by Priory Farm to continue on the footpath towards Selborne.

After walking through a portion of Coombe Wood and past some ponds, you arrive at the end of the Long Lythe which is National Trust property. Follow the path along both Long and Short Lythes to emerge in the meadow below Selborne Church. Climb the hill and go through the churchyard to the Plestor. Turn left along Selborne High Street to arrive back at the *Queens Hotel*.

Notes on the walk — Headley to Selborne

Next to the church stands the old Rectory, which had been under repair in 1830. It was described in 1783 as: 'A very good house, consisting of two parlours and hall, a kitchen and pantry on the ground floor; four bed-chambers, six garrets, four underground cellars, with a brew-house, milk-house, and other convenient offices; also of two spacious barns, a stable, cow-pens, granary, waggon-house, fuel-house, ash-house, etc. The gardens, yard and rick-yard amount to about one and three-quarter acres'.

The Holme School takes its name from Dr George Holme, Rector of Headley 1718–65, who had given the parish a school in 1755. The original building stands beside the Village Green.

Church Lane takes its name from the fact that it forms part of the old track from Headley church towards the outlying parts of the parish on the way to Farnham. You will follow it, with some modern diversions, as far as Trottsford.

Huntingford Farm was built around 1774, according to a rent-roll of that date which has an entry for John Huntingford of: *"one close called Church-field with a tenement thereon newly erected containing 4 acres lying at Lackmore-cross on the south part of Curtis Lane"* – we assume it is this building. It was thatched until 1959, when the roof was lost in a fire.

The aqueduct over the River Wey is part of an extensive system of channels which would have extended along the river in 1830, through this parish and beyond, to regulate the watermeadows. Water was diverted from the river by a weir into a header ditch, which had a number of sluices along its length allowing water to be spread evenly over the meadow in a controlled fashion before draining back into the river. This system added nutrients to the land, allowing early crops of fodder to be produced, and a second cut to be made later in the year.

As you arrive at Pickett's Hill road, note the footpath straight ahead which marks the old route to Farnham prior to the building of the turnpike.

Near the point where you cross the A325 at Sleaford there once stood a tollhouse, opposite the *New Inn*. It was eventually removed when the road was widened. The *New Inn* itself consists of a 'new' section facing the turnpike, and an older section behind facing the road which existed prior to the turnpike's construction. *[The New Inn site was redeveloped in 2002, retaining the existing buildings]*

In crossing the River Slea you pass from Headley into Kingsley parish. There is a stone set into the west side of the old bridge indicating this.

At Kingsley Pond, note the area on higher ground to your right behind the church which was called 'Kingsley Green' on old maps. It was at Kingsley Green, we are told, that Holdaway "called out ten persons as the representatives of the ten parishes of which the labourers had formed your dangerous and illegal assembly" and shared out the spoils of the day. The church would not have been here at the time, having been built only in 1876.

In reality, the various men from 'ten parishes' must have made their separate ways home from here in several different directions—but we follow a probable route of those heading back to the centre of Selborne.

Kingsley Mill is of some antiquity, and legend says that it may even have been the mill that Geoffrey Chaucer had in mind when writing his Miller's Tale! His son Thomas was Lord Warden of Woolmer and Alice Holt Forests at the end of the 14th century, and is said to be buried nearby at East Worldham, where he lived.

The disused railway viaduct belongs to the spur from Bentley to Bordon, opened in 1905 and closed in the 1960s.

Oakhanger is a hamlet in the parish of Selborne, and so to some of the 'Selborne' rioters it would be home. In particular, the Heighes brothers lived here. For others, there were still a few miles to travel cross country.

Priory Farm is on the site of Selborne Priory, closed in 1484 due to bad debts, and the stones reused for various local and not-so-local building projects.

The Long Lythe and Short Lythe (pronounced 'Lith') are footpaths which were mentioned in the writings of Gilbert White.

Within the church of St Mary, Selborne, is displayed the collar of vicar Cobbold's large mastiff, which he bought to protect himself after the riot.

The Great Yew of Selborne sadly blew down in 1990, and never recovered. According to Mrs Cowburn, men climbed into its branches on the evening of Sunday 21st November 1830 to overlook the vicarage and make sure Cobbold would not get away in the night.

The Queen's Hotel was, in 1830, stated as being the only public house in Selborne. At that time it was called the Compasses, or some say the Goat and Compasses which may be a corruption of 'God encompasseth us'. Robert Holdaway was the landlord here until about a year before the riot. It was renamed the Queens Inn in 1839.

120

Calendar of Events

ᘒᘒᘒ

November 1830

Sa 20   Selborne: Shots fired at the Harrisons
Mo 22   Selborne: Workhouse sacked, Cobbold mobbed
             Liphook disturbance
Tu 23   Headley/Kingsley events
We 24   Wyck threshing machine damaged
Th 25   Budd reports 13 taken to Liphook

Dates of warrants: *Committed by:*

Fr 26   Thomas Robinson   Headley workhouse   *Budd*
             Robert Holdaway   Headley workhouse   *Budd*
             Thomas Marshall   Headley / Robbery   *Budd*
             William Bicknell   Headley workhouse   *Budd*
Mo 29   William Heighes   Wyck threshing machine   *RN Lee*
             Thomas Heighes   Wyck threshing machine   *RN Lee*
             John Newland   Mobbing vicar   *Knight/Hugonin*
Tu 30   John Heath   Headley workhouse   *Hugonin*

December 1830

Th 2   Henry James   Headley workhouse   *Budd*
             James Painter   Headley workhouse   *Budd*
             William Bright   Robbery in Headley   *Budd*
             Thomas Hoare   Selborne workhouse   *JBC*
Sa 4   Matthew Triggs   Headley workhouse   *JBC*
             Thomas Harding   Headley workhouse   *JBC*
             Henry Bone   Selborne workhouse   *JBC*
             Aaron Harding   Headley workhouse   *JBC*
             John Cobb   Selborne workhouse   *JBC*
Mo 6   John Trimming   Mobbing vicar   *Hugonin*
Tu 14   William Hoare   Selborne workhouse   *Hugonin*
We 15   Benjamin Smith   Selborne workhouse   *Hugonin*
             Robert Bennett   Selborne workhouse   *Hugonin*
             John Kingshott   Robbery in Kingsley   *Budd*
Mo 20   Special Commission started work in Winchester
Th 23   Trial: Selborne workhouse

---

* *Note that the dates on the warrants are almost certainly later than the dates of actual arrest. In Liphook, where Henry Budd stated in a letter to John Bonham-Carter (JBC) on 25th November that he and John Coles had already 'taken' 13 men, the warrants for five of the men he named are not dated until over a week later.*

Mo	27	Trial: Headley workhouse
We	29	Trial: Mobbing Selborne vicar
Th	30	Sentences passed: Holdaway 'left for execution'

January 1831

Sa	1	Cowburn wrote to Vaughan
Mo	3	Cowburn wrote to Lord Melbourne
		Cobbold went to see Lord Melbourne
Th	6	Melbourne replied to Cowburn
Fr	7	Wellington wrote to Cowburn
Sa	8	Holdaway respited till 5th February
Tu	11	Thomas Heighes transferred to hulk *York*
We	12	James Bridger wrote to Cowburn
Sa	15	Execution of Cook and Cooper
Mo	31	Holdaway's counsel wrote to Lord Melbourne

February 1831

Dates transferred to hulk York:			*Sailed in:*
Th	3	Henry James	*Eleanor*
Sa	5	Matthew Triggs	*Eleanor*
		Aaron Harding	*Eleanor*
Su	6	Thomas Heighes sailed in *Eliza*;	arr. Tasmania 29 May
Tu	8	John Heath	*Eleanor*
We	9	Robert Holdaway	*Eleanor*
		John Kingshott	*Proteus*
Th	10	Thomas Harding	*Proteus*
		James Painter	Not transported
Sa	19	*Eleanor* sailed	Arrived NSW on 25th June

March 1831

Tu	1	James Painter	Transferred to hulk *Hardy*

April 1831

Th	14	*Proteus* sailed	Arrived Tasmania on 4th August

Acknowledgements

The following general texts were consulted:—

J. Curtis, *History of Alton* (1896)
W.W. Capes, *Rural Life in Hampshire* (1901)
W.H. Hudson, *Hampshire Days* (1902)
J.L. & B. Hammond, *The Village Labourer 1760–1832* (1911)
Victoria History of the Counties of England (1911)
G.D.H. Cole & R. Postgate, *The Common People 1746–1946* (rev 1946)
David Cecil, *Lord M.* (1954)
M. & C.H.B. Quennell, *A History of Everyday Things in England* (rev 1961)
E.J. Hobsbawm & G. Rudé, *Captain Swing* (1968)
Bob Bushaway, *By Rite* (1982)
Robert Hughes, *The Fatal Shore* (1987)
Aileen M Roberson, *The Rockley Manner* (1989)
Jill Chambers, *Rebels of the Fields* (1995)
Jill Chambers, *Hampshire Machine Breakers* (rev 1996)
David Kent & Norma Townsend, *Joseph Mason* (1996)
Edward W Northwood, *The Life & Work of William Harper* (1999)
Ian Webb, *Road's End: Building the Great North Road* (2000)
David Kent & Norma Townsend, *The Convicts of the 'Eleanor'* (2002)

… and websites too numerous to list.

References from Records Offices:—

Public Records Office:
　H017/50 Hp41, Petitions: *Letters from Holdaway's counsel
　　to Lord Melbourne*

Hampshire Records Office:
　9M74/1: *The Revolt of the Hampshire Labourers and its Causes,
　　1812–31*, Thesis by A M Colson – written 1937
　14M50/1–4: *Calendar of Prisoners at the Special Commission, etc*
　32M66 P06, P08: *Selborne Parish registers*
　44M69 J9/77: *Resolutions of Alton vestry 1830*
　94M72 F15–16: *Charge to the Grand Jury, etc*

Centre for Kentish Studies:
　U1127: *Correspondence of William Cowburn Esq*

Other material:
　Trial transcripts, and reports from *The Times*.
　Registers of Magdalen College, Oxford.

Illustrations and Maps:—

The Plestor in Selborne: The Wakes Museum, Selborne
Poster issued by small farmers of Headley in May 1822: Joyce Stevens
Robert Holdaway's signature in Selborne vestry minutes: Ted Yates
Map of Selborne in 1843: traced from Tithe map, Hampshire County
    Records Office
Plan of Selborne Workhouse: Derived from a diagram in the Selborne
    Rate and Vestry Book of 1836
The Anchor, Liphook in the 1800s: Roger Newman
Map of local area circa 1815: Hampshire County Records Office/ Ordnance
    Survey
A Horse-driven Threshing Machine circa 1830: Rural History Centre,
    University of Reading
Headley Rectory: sketch by Mick Borra from artwork of the period
Cowburn correspondence: Centre for Kentish Studies, Maidstone
Map of Headley in 1855: Headley Parish Council
Headley Church before 1836: sketch by Hester Whittle from artwork of
    the period
Personal photographs from descendants of the Rioters
Sketch of Headley Workhouse rear gates by Dil Williamson
Local photographs by the author

For other local material and also a great deal of their time spent in talking to me, I have to thank in particular:—

Joyce Stevens, founder of The Headley Society
Ted Yates, of Selborne
Paul Roberts, of Selborne
Natalie Mees of Selborne
Laurence Giles, of the Bramshott & Liphook Preservation Society
Tracey Jones, sometime Head of History at Mill Chase Community
    School, Bordon
Sue Allden, of Headley
The late John Ellis, of Headley Mill
Mr & Mrs Broom, owners of *Headley Grange*
Julia Fry (now Mayo), sometime of East Hampshire District Council

And the families of the rioters:—

See entries in 'Personalities' section above.

In particular, I would like to extend my thanks to Geof Watts,
descendant of Aaron Harding, for his persistence in tracking down
many Australian records for me.

Commemorations

ᘏᘓᘏ

On the morning of St George's Day, 23rd April 1994, a group of some 20 people gathered in the High Street at Headley. Thankfully, the earlier rain had cleared giving rise to a bright spring day.

The party included descendants of four of the rioters: Keith Holdaway *(Robert Holdaway)*, Marjorie Burwood *(Aaron Harding)*, Phil Viney *(Matthew Triggs)* and Jean Vivian *(John Newland)*, along with members of their families. Jill Chambers (author of *Hampshire Machine Breakers*) and representatives from the two villages and the cast of the play *This Bloody Crew* were also present.

L to R: Phil Viney, John Owen Smith, Jean Vivian, Ann Viney, Nigel Mulcaster at a meeting of the Selborne Association, October 1996

We walked from the *Holly Bush* inn down to Headley workhouse, the path that Robert Holdaway had taken in desperation more than 163 years before, when he discovered his Selborne men had gone back on their word and attacked the place while he was meeting the Headley rector and farmers inside the pub.

In the grounds of the workhouse, now a private house called Headley Grange, we planted a cutting of the famous Selborne Yew Tree in memory of

Robert and the other rioters who had been transported for their actions at this place.

We then retired for lunch at the *Crown Inn*, where Matthew Triggs' wife had passed her last days, and met Norma Townsend from Australia, over here researching the history of the Swing Rioters transported to NSW.

Many notes and addresses were swapped in what we felt had been a happy and successful occasion, and probably unique in the history of the 'Swing' riots.

ᘰᘰᘰ

At the October 1996 meeting of the Selborne Association, John Owen Smith brought along descendants of three of the men convicted for the Selborne Workhouse Riot of 1830—Robert Holdaway, John Newland and Matthew Triggs—to speak about how the families had fared after their breadwinners had been imprisoned or transported. *(See photo on previous page)*

Transcripts of what they told the audience have been included elsewhere in this book.

Echoes of a Trumpet

by Jean Newland *(Jean Vivian)*

After the labourers' riots of 1830, the village of Selborne was in turmoil.

Whole families were left without breadwinners when husbands and sons were transported to the other side of the world for their part in the uprising. But John Newland — the legendary ring-leader and 'Trumpeter' — was released after only six months custody in Winchester gaol.

In this book his great-great-granddaughter serves us fact laced with supposition, to bring us a story of two young people caught up in the bitterness of a conflict which had happened before they were even born.

Only the strength of their love for each other can overcome such a legacy — the strained echoes of a trumpet, still stirring discontent through the years.

ISBN 1-873855-30-3 November 1998, paperback, 148pp

Dramatisations

The author of this book has written both a stage play and a radio play covering the events of the riot and their aftermath.

The stage play, which began the author's involvement in the subject, was first performed in October 1993 under the title *This Bloody Crew* – which was William Cobbett's description of the *Times* newspaper and the government of the time.

Aaron Harding (Tony Grant), Matthew Triggs (Nick Benham) and Robert Holdaway (Steve Povey) in the 1993 production of 'This Bloody Crew'

It covers the events of the riot during the two days in Selborne and Headley, and the trial of the ringleaders.

The radio play, which was broadcast in May 1994, takes up the story after the trial and centres on William Cowburn's successful efforts to spare Robert Holdaway from the gallows. It is titled *Condemned*, or *Not Fit to Live in England* – the latter phrase being Cowburn's comment on Holdaway and the rioters about to be transported.

Riot! or ***This Bloody Crew*** – *ISBN 1-873855-01-X paperback*
Condemned! or ***Not Fit to Live in England*** *available on audio cassette,*
*   or as a script.*
For details and performance rights of both these plays, contact the author at the address shown at the end of this book.

Books relating to the history of Headley

All Tanked Up—*the Canadians in Headley during World War II*
A story of the benign 'invasion' of Headley by Canadian tank regiments over a period of four years, told from the point of view of both Villagers and Canadians. Includes many personal reminiscences and illustrations.
ISBN 1-873855-00-1 May 1994, paperback, 48pp, illustrations plus maps.

Headley Miscellany—a series of booklets containing a compilation of historical facts and stories about Headley parish from several contributors.
The Headley Society, 1999 onwards, paperback, 44pp each issue, illustrated.

To the Ar and Back—*an historical stroll around Headley and Arford*
Joyce Stevens tells us the history of forty-seven locations within a mile of the centre of Headley. Illustrated with line drawings by Mick Borra.
The Headley Society, reprinted April 1994, paperback, 26pp, illus + map.

A Parcel of Gold for Edith—*letters from Australia to Headley 1853–1875*
"Hidden in a tin that had once held Andies Candies, I found seven faded letters which revealed the life story of a remarkable woman, my great-great aunt." Joyce Stevens tells us the result of her 30-year search into the identity of one of Australia's Pioneer Women.
ISBN 1-873855-36-2 November 2001, paperback, 102pp, illustrated.

Headley's Past in Pictures — *a tour of the parish in old photographs*
Headley as it was in the first half of the 20th century. In this book you are taken on an illustrated tour of the parish by means of three journeys – the first around the centre of Headley and Arford, the second to Headley Down and beyond, and the third along the River Wey and its tributaries. In doing so, we venture occasionally outside today's civil parish boundaries – but that too is all part of the history of Headley.
ISBN 1-873855-27-3 December 1999, paperback, 128pp,
over 100 photographs, plus historical notes and maps of area.

The Southern Wey—*a guide, by The River Wey Trust*
Covers the Southern River Wey from its source near Haslemere through Headley parish to Tilford where it joins the northern branch. Gives fascinating details on geology, industry, landscape and ecology of our area.
ISBN 0-9514187-0-X reprinted Jan 1990, paperback, 46pp, well illustrated

/contd ...

Some Ancient Churches in North East Hampshire
—an illustrated collection of notes
Twelve fascinating churches in the north east corner of Hampshire are described. A map on the back cover guides you through the picturesque lanes of the area, and 33 photographs give both exterior and interior views of each church. As well as Headley, the book includes Alton, Bentley, Binsted, Bramshott, Froyle, Hartley Mauditt, Holybourne, Kingsley, Selborne, and East & West Worldham. A short glossary is included for those unfamiliar with some of the architectural terms used. Suitable size for the pocket.
ISBN 1-873855-11-7 April 1995, paperback, 28pp, illustrations plus map.

On the Trail of Flora Thompson—*beyond Candleford Green*
The author of *Lark Rise to Candleford* worked in Grayshott post office from 1898–1901, while it was still in the parish of Headley. A local historian investigates the people and places she would have seen here at that time.
ISBN 1-873855-24-9 May 1997, paperback, 144pp, illustrations plus maps.

Heatherley—*by Flora Thompson—her sequel to the 'Lark Rise' trilogy*
This is the book which Flora Thompson wrote about her time in Grayshott. It is the 'missing' fourth part to her *Lark Rise to Candleford* collection in which 'Laura Goes Further'. Illustrated with chapter-heading line drawings by Hester Whittle. Introduction by Ann Mallinson.
ISBN 1-873855-29-X Sept 1998, paperback, 178pp, illustrations plus maps.

Grayshott—*the story of a Hampshire village* by J. H. (Jack) Smith
ISBN 1-873855-38-9 Originally published 1976 – republished 2002

The River Running By—*a history of Standford*
Author: John Warren—Publisher: Standford Hill Methodist Church (1986)

Out of print:—

Headley 1066–1966
Author: Canon Tudor Jones—Publisher: the author (1966)
— now being serialised in issues of the *Headley Miscellany*

John Owen Smith, publisher:—
Tel/Fax: (01428) 712892
E-mail: wordsmith@headley-village.com
Web Site: www.headley-village.com/wordsmith

Index